Basketball's
Motion Game
Offenses

Basketball's Motion Game Offenses

Harry L. "Mike" Harkins

MacGregor Sports Education
Waukesha, Wisconsin

Library of Congress Cataloging-in-Publication Data

Harkins, Harry L.
  Basketball's motion game offenses.

  1. Basketball—Offense.   2. Basketball—Coaching.
I. Title
GV889.H3   1987   796.32′32   87-2720

ISBN 0-941175-01-4

Printed in United States of America

Dedication

This book is dedicated to my wife, Grace, who, along with being the love of my life, has been a working partner in the books I have written. Without her meticulous efforts on the diagrams and hours spent typing, they might never have been completed.

Acknowledgments

Grateful appreciation is expressed to the sources of my basketball knowledge, including:

Russ Estey and Mike Krino, my high school coaches.
Russ Beichly and Red Cochrane, my college coaches.
Buck Hyser, who gave me my first coaching job.
Andy Golobic, who fostered my love of the game.
And the players who have played on my teams.

A final note of thanks goes to my number one fans (and granddaughters) Shellee Ann and Jamee Cameron Harkins.

How the Motion Game Offenses
Can Help Your Team

The title of this book, *Basketball's Motion Game Offenses,* refers to motion-oriented offenses in general and not to a specific offense. It is the result of my experience with such innovative motion offenses as the weave, the shuffle, reverse action, the passing game, and the flex.

Although motion game offenses have been a part of the game since Dr. Harold C. Carlson originated the weave, the prominence they now enjoy is a recent development.

In the 1950s and 1960s, basketball was a high-scoring, free-flowing, wide open game. Offensively, most teams attempted to fast break and when this was stymied, turned to set plays that resulted in quick shots. The eventual change in offensive philosophy was necessitated by the development of clear, concise, pressure-and-help man-to-man defensive rules. They made stationary set plays very difficult to execute. Evidence of this is found in what happened when the impact of this defense hit the N.B.A. Officials there, fearing it would give defense the edge and lower scores, made a rule prohibiting an offside defender from having both feet in the lane for more than 2.9 seconds. College and high school coaches reacted in a different fashion. They developed motion game offenses that attempted to negate the pressure-and-help rules with movement. Since the shot options of these offensive plans were not as pronounced as those of set plays, coaches began to stress disciplined shot selection. Perhaps the pioneer offense in this regard was the "passing game" which moved the defense and confused their pressure-and-help assignments. It also provided for disciplined shot selection with a rule stating "make at least four passes before shooting unless an unmolested lay-up shot develops." The passing game was followed by the more structured flex motion and eventually by a myriad of "motion game" offenses.

This book contains offenses from the 1-4, 1-2-2, 1-3-1, 2-3, 2-1-2, and high post stack sets. Among the offenses are complete motion games in which all five players interchange, and abbreviated motion games that tend to keep players in their areas of expertise. An example of the latter would be an offense in which the two big players occupy the lane area, and the three smaller men create motion on the offensive perimeter.

Each chapter consists of a description of the ideal personnel for a given offense, the basic motion, pressure relievers to combat the pressure-help defense, auxiliary plays to meet specific situations, and tips on how this man-to-man offense may be adapted to function versus zone defenses.

The motion game offenses are presented in the following manner:

Chapter 1 The Moving Stack Offense. This offense is a five-man motion built around the stack maneuver. It contains many post-up situations in the context of a motion game that attempts to take away the offside help. The net result is an abundance of high percentage shots.

Chapter 2 The Variable Offside Cut Motion Game. This motion is built around a series of offside screens that are made each time the offense is executed on a given side. They are described as variable because the order in which they are run is not always the same.

Chapter 3 The Flex-Plus Motion. The Flex-Plus Motion is an extension of the very popular flex offense. It has all the attributes of the flex and adds a lob pass option and a double screen.

Chapter 4 The Guard Loop Three-Play Motion. This is a very basic offensive plan. However, it has been used at many levels of competition and with great success. It consists of a single pattern with three options and may be used with very few adjustments against zone defenses.

Chapter 5 The Passing Game Overload Motion. The Passing Game Overload Motion is versatile in that it may be run as a five-man interchangeable plan, or as an abbreviated continuity that keeps the three small men on the perimeter and the two big men inside. It uses the functional pass-and-screen-away maneuver identified with the passing game and offers an innovative offensive wrinkle by utilizing an overloaded set.

Chapter 6 The 1-3-1 Wheel Motion Game. This motion is based on three circular patterns that lead to set plays. These patterns move the defense in a probing fashion that leads to high percentage shots.

Chapter 7 The Lob Motion. This lob-oriented motion involves many basic play components. They include the UCLA slash cut, an offside screen, and a post-to-post backscreen leading to a lob pass.

Chapter 8 The De Paul Cut Motion Offense. This motion is a method of utilizing a big man within the context of motion. It is based on the De Paul forward-to-guard lob play.

Chapter 9 A Disciplined Flex Control Motion. This plan is for the team that is willing and able to play control ball. It points out and utilizes the advantages of working for high percentage shot selection.

This book offers variations of motion games that will enable your team to frustrate the proponents of the pressure-help, man-to-man defenses. You may choose to adopt one of these plans in its entirety, or use this material as a playbook from which to select individual motion continuities, or set plays, to add to your present offensive system. Whichever you choose, I hope that through this work I have made some contribution to your success in the often frustrating, but always challenging and invigorating profession of coaching basketball.

Mike Harkins

CONTENTS

CHAPTER 1

The Moving Stack Offense

The Moving Stack Offense is a five-man motion game that features high percentage shots. The design of the movement takes away the offside defensive help and results in many one-on-one "post-ups" in the ballside post area. It may be adapted for use against zone defenses.

PERSONNEL ALIGNMENT

Since the offense is a five-man motion game, it is ideal for a team without a dominant big man. It is a very functional plan for the team possessing a great many "in-between size players" who would be classified as large guards or small forwards. Players of this size often have problems on teams running nonmotion plays from a standard 2-3 set. However, in a motion offense featuring "post-up" opportunities, their skills can often be fully utilized. The motion begins with the · best ballhandler (1) at the point and a double stack with the two best post players at the top of the stacks (see (4) and (5) in Diagram 1-1) and the best jump shooters (2) and (3) in the bottom.

THE BASIC MOTION

Player (1) must be the team's top ballhandler because he controls the ball until the inside men in the stack, (2) and (3), pop out of the downscreens set by (5) and (4), and an entry pass can be made.

In Diagram 1-2, (1) chooses to pass to (3). After the pass, (1) screens down for the offside post man (4), who moves to the point. This motion takes away the offside help's primary helper (X4) and permits (5) to play one-on-one in the ballside post area.

If (3) does not have a shot, and (5) is not open, the next pass option is to (4) at the point. Player (4) looks first for a shot; second, to (5) in the post; and third, to (1), who received a downscreen from (2). See Diagram 1-3.

In Diagram 1-3, it should be stressed that (4) can very often get the ball inside to (5). When (3) had the ball, (5)'s defender (X5) was either fronting (5) or at least playing him to deny the pass. When (4) gets the pass from (3), he often has an excellent angle from which to pass to (5) for a power lay-up shot. The fact that X1 and X2 are engaged in a stack play diminishes the possibility of their helping X5.

After (4) passes to (1) coming out of the stack, he screens down for (5) who cuts to the point and the same options now exist on the other side of the court. See Diagram 1-4.

Dribble Chase Play

When you want variety, or when the initial entry pass is being denied, (1) may dribble at one of the wing men, (2) or (3), and key the dribble chase play. In

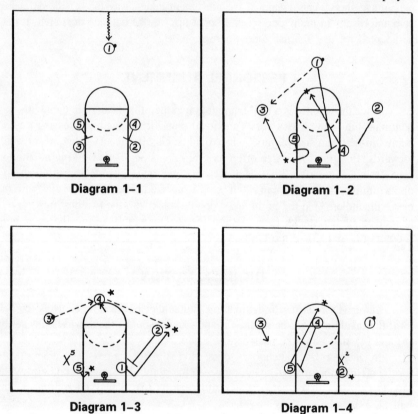

Diagram 1-1   Diagram 1-2

Diagram 1-3   Diagram 1-4

Diagram 1-5, (1) chooses to dribble at (2). This chases (2) down and across the lane. It also tells (4) to screen away for (5), who cuts to the ballside looking for a pass from (1).

Seeing this action, the offside wing man (3) moves down toward the lane. After screening for (5), (4) cuts to the head of the key. See Diagram 1-6.

If (5) is not open, (1) passes to (4) at the point. Player (4) may then: (A) pass inside to (5) who has inside position on his defender X5, or (B) look for (2) coming out of (3)'s downscreen of the offside stack play. See Diagram 1-7.

If the pass is made to (5), he powers up for a lay-up. If (4) chooses to pass to (2), (2) may shoot or look inside for (3). If nothing develops, the motion will go on with (4) screening down for (5), and then (1) screening down for (4). See Diagrams 1-8 and 1-9.

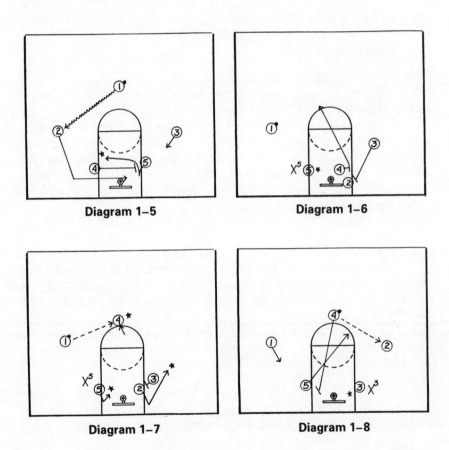

Diagram 1–5   Diagram 1–6

Diagram 1–7   Diagram 1–8

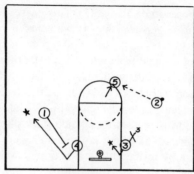

Diagram 1–9

Passes to the Post

Point-to-Post Pass

When this motion is being run, passes into the post always result in split plays. Diagram 1-10 shows what occurs when point man (1) passes to post man (4), as he breaks high. This pass keys (2) to backdoor his defender.

Player (4) looks first for (2) on the backdoor cut. Player (1) comes down and screens for (2), who stops and then cuts to the wing area. See Diagram 1-11. Player (3) becomes the new point man as (1) rolls inside and then clears to the offside wing area. See Diagram 1-12.

From there, if no shot is forthcoming, the ball can be passed to (3) at the point and a new play may be run.

Wing Pass to Post

When a pass is made from a wing to the post (as the pass from (2) to (4) in Diagram 1-13) a split play is again run. Player (2) moves out to screen (1), who comes to the ball; (2) then rolls down the middle, and (3) assumes the point position.

The simple movement of these two split plays has scoring potential and keeps the defenders on (1) and (2) busy enough to prevent them from sagging on the post man (4).

DRIBBLE CLEARS AS PRESSURE RELIEVERS

When this offense is being run, two passes in particular tend to be denied by the defense. They are: (A) when point man (1) attempts to pass to either wing man, and (B) when a wing man attempts to return the ball to the point.

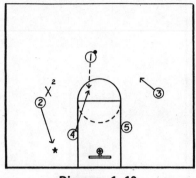

Diagram 1–10

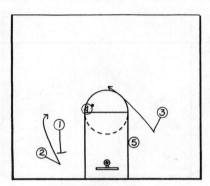

Diagram 1–11

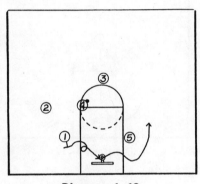

Diagram 1–12

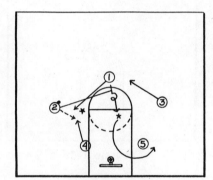

Diagram 1–13

Point-to-Wing Pass Denial

We have already established that when the dribble entry is used on the initial phase of a play, the Dribble Chase Play is run. However, once the offense has been initiated and the point man dribbles at his wing man, a simple position exchange occurs. Diagram 1-14 shows (1) dribbling at (2). This tells him to clear down and around post man (4) and to the point. In effect, (1) and (2) have exchanged positions. Player (1) would then pass to (2) and the basic continuity would follow. See Diagrams 1-15 and 1-16.

Having two types of point-to-wing dribble plays may seem complicated. However, we have found it to our advantage to teach both, but either will suffice on its own.

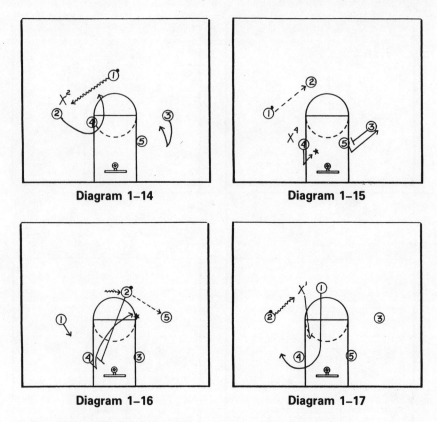

Diagram 1–14   Diagram 1–15

Diagram 1–16   Diagram 1–17

Wing-to-Point Denial

In Diagram 1-17, wing man (2) is unable to pass to point man (1), so he dribbles at him and, in effect, changes position with him. Player (1) clears down the lane to replace (2) at the wing.

From there, the continuity goes on. See Diagrams 1-18 and 1-19.

AUXILIARY PLAYS

The following auxiliary plays may be used to add depth to the offense as the season progresses, or to take advantage of specific situations.

Lob Play

At the moment in the basic motion when the man at the head of the key ((4) in Diagram 1-20) passes to the stack side and screens down for the offside post man, the lob play may be inserted. This is accomplished by having the offside post man (5) make a premature cut to the free throw line area. Player (4) then attempts to use (5) to rub off his man and receive a lob pass from (2).

In the event (4) is not open, (5) pops out to the head of the key and the basic motion is resumed. See Diagram 1-21.

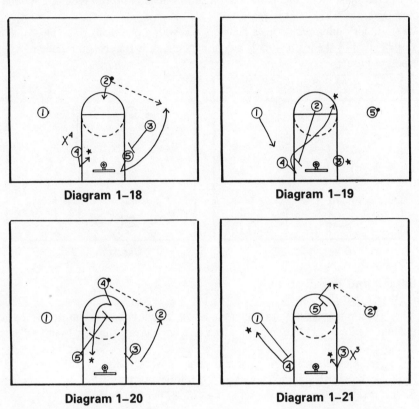

Diagram 1–18   Diagram 1–19

Diagram 1–20   Diagram 1–21

Two-Man Front Option

If a team lacks a dominant point guard who can bring the ball upcourt and control it until a play can be initiated, the following option may be utilized:

Guards (1) and (2) share the task of bringing the ball upcourt. A guard-to-guard pass is then made (as from (1) to (2) in Diagram 1-22). Guard (1) cuts through and may: (A) loop around post man (4), or (B) loop around post man (5) and wing man (3), who is stacked inside (5).

A. Around the Post Man (4)

After passing to (2), (1) chooses to loop around post man (4). This tells (3) that he should go opposite (1) by popping out of (5)'s downscreen. See Diagram 1-22. The players are then in position to run the basic motion.

B. Around the Stack

This time (1) passes to (2) and cuts around the stack. This tells (3) to go opposite (1)'s cut by moving across the lane and utilizing (4)'s downscreen to pop out to the wing area. The players are again in position to run the basic motion. See Diagram 1-23.

Either option results in a double stack with a one-man front. This option may be used by the team without a dominant guard that wishes to run the moving stack offense.

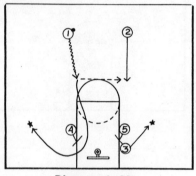 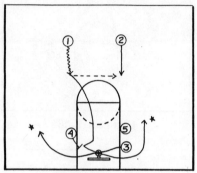

Diagram 1-22   **Diagram 1-23**

Screen-and-Roll Option

The point man ((1) in Diagram 1-24) calls this option during the basic motion. He keys it by passing to a stack side and cutting directly to the ballside corner.

This cut tells (5) to step out and screen for (3). Player (3) dribbles off (5) and looks for either a jump shot or for (5) rolling. At the same time, (2) screens down for (4), who pops to the wing area. See Diagram 1-25.

If (3) does not have a shot and (5) is not open, (3) passes to (4), and the basic continuity is resumed. See Diagram 1-26.

This option permits a team to interject a screen-and-roll maneuver and then return to the basic pattern without really interrupting the flow of the offense.

Overshifted Post-Up Play

When the post man ((4) in Diagram 1-27) can score on his defender at a very high percentage rate and a *quick* basket is needed, the Overshifted Post-Up Play may be run.

This play is keyed by the offside post man (5) who, on a post-to-wing pass, breaks to the ballside corner. This clears the defense's primary helper X5.

Seeing (5)'s cut, (1) moves to the offside head of the key and (3) flashes to the ballside high post area, as (2) attempts to get the ball to (4). See Diagram 1-28.

If X4 plays behind (4), he receives a pass from (2) for a one-on-one play. See Diagram 1-29. If (4) is being fronted by X4, a lob pass may be used because the offside defensive help has been cleared. See Diagram 1-30.

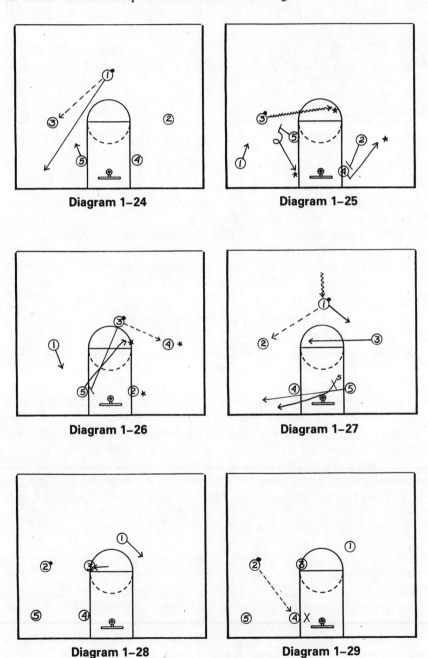

Diagram 1–24

Diagram 1–25

Diagram 1–26

Diagram 1–27

Diagram 1–28

Diagram 1–29

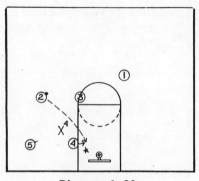 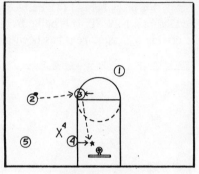

Diagram 1–30   **Diagram 1–31**

When (4) is fronted, (2) may also pass to (3) in the high post. This will change the passing angle and leave (4) inside X4 to receive a pass from (3) for a power lay-up shot. See Diagram 1-31.

Note that in all three of the options (1) has taken his defender to a position that disallows any help on (3) or (4).

Player (2) may cancel this play at any time by dribbling at (1) and keying the basic motion game. See Diagrams 1-32 and 1-33.

VERSUS ZONE DEFENSES

Lob Option

Against zones, it is best to run the Lob Option and adjust its timing. In Diagram 1-34 (1) brings the ball upcourt and stops. This keys (2) and (3) to break out of their respective stacks. Player (1) chooses to pass to (2). This tells the offside post man (5) to break to a high post position. If (2) can get the ball to (5), either (4) or the offside wing man (3) are very often open.

At this point, (1) can cut through to the open low post area or stay out front and move the ball with (2) and (3), as shown in Diagrams 1-35 and 1-36.

Player (1) may cut through any time the ball is on the side of the low post man (4). So this time, as he passes to (2), he cuts over (5) to the open offside low post. This tells (5) to move to the point and (3) to screen down for (1). See Diagram 1-37.

Player (2) passes to (5), who reverses it to (1), coming around (3)'s downscreen. Player (3) attempts to pin the one defender nearest the play inside the lane. Bringing big man (5) out front has an added advantage in that he may have been able to throw a two-hand overhead pass over the defenders to (4) in the heart of the zone. See Diagram 1-38.

Player (5)'s pass to (1) tells the offside post man (4) to break to a high post position and from there the same options prevail. See Diagram 1-39.

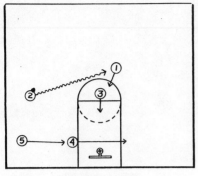

Diagram 1–32

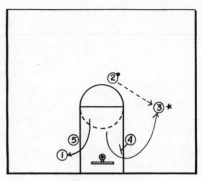

Diagram 1–33

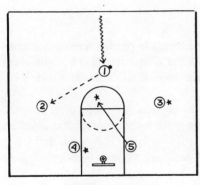

Diagram 1–34

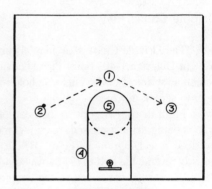

Diagram 1–35

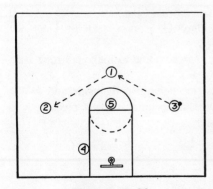

Diagram 1–36

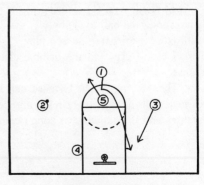

Diagram 1–37

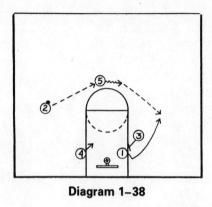

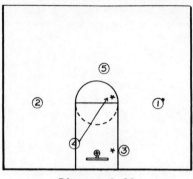

Diagram 1–38   **Diagram 1–39**

Dribble Chase Play

The Dribble Chase Play may also be adapted to provide an excellent zone play. In Diagram 1-40, point man (1) dribbles at wing man (2). This tells (4) to screen away for (5), who cuts to a hole in the zone. It also tells the offside wing man to screen down.

From there, (4) pops to the head of the key and the onside wing man (2), who is being dribble-chased, may: (A) move to the ballside corner and create an overload (see Diagram 1-41), or (B) cut across the lane. This would tell (1) to quickly reverse the ball to (2) by way of (4), and catch the zone overshifted. Note that (3) screened the nearest zone defender. See Diagram 1-42.

Again, it should be stressed that (4) is tall and may be able to throw over the smaller front zone players and directly to (5).

This concept may also be used on a wing-to-point dribble. In Diagram 1-43, (2) dribbles at (1), whose clearing cut creates an overload.

In Diagrams 1-44 and 1-45, (2) dribbles at (1) and an overshifted screen • play will result with (1) clearing to the side opposite (2)'s pass to (3). Player (3) then reverses the ball to (1) by way of (2). Player (4) screens down for (1) and the result is an overshifted screen play.

The lob play and the dribble chase play combine to make a strong zone offense.

The Moving Stack Offense can test the defense both inside and on the perimeter. It has pressure-relieving devices to counter today's pressure-help defenses and is adaptable to zone defenses.

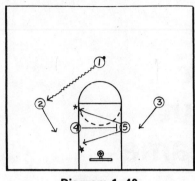

Diagram 1–40

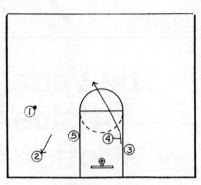

Diagram 1–41

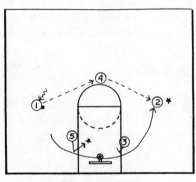

Diagram 1–42

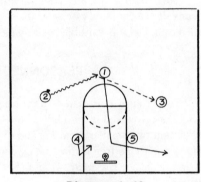

Diagram 1–43

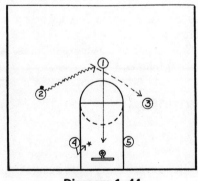

Diagram 1–44

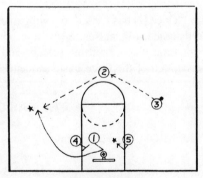

Diagram 1–45

CHAPTER 2

The Variable Offside Cut Motion Game

This motion offense is built around offside screens, and cuts off the screens. It is a continuity because the same cuts are made each time the offense is turned over, and it is variable because the order of the cuts is not always the same.

PERSONNEL ALIGNMENT

The offense is initiated from a double stack and a point guard. The two stacks are composed of two big men ((4) and (5) in Diagram 2-1) on top of the stacks, and two smaller men, (2) and (3), at the bottom of the stacks. Players (2) and (3) pop to the free throw line extended as point man (1) penetrates to a safe passing distance. Big men (4) and (5) then post up in their respective low post positions.

Offside Screens and Cuts

Once (1) has passed to a wing man (as to (2) in Diagram 2-2), the post man on that side, (4), moves to the high post area.

From there the same screens and cuts are made in varying sequences. A description of the three basic sequences (plays) follows.

THE BASIC MOTIONS

Play #1—Wing First Play

As wing man (2) in Diagram 2-3 receives the ball from point man (1), the offside wing man (3) cuts off the low post man on his side, (5), and to the ballside low post area vacated by (4)'s move to the high post area.

In Diagram 2-3, (2) should pass to (3) when he is open under the basket. If (3) is not open, he clears to the ballside corner. Seeing this, (4) screens away for (5), who cuts to a ballside post position. See Diagram 2-4.

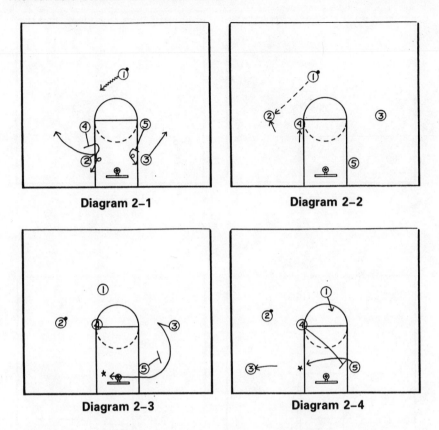

Diagram 2-1   Diagram 2-2

Diagram 2-3   Diagram 2-4

Player (1) then screens down for (4) who moves to the head of the key; (2) may now pass to (5) moving to the post for a one-on-one play or to (4) moving out front. See Diagram 2-5.

Balancing Move

When the pass is made to (4), (2) moves to the offside wing and (3) moves to replace him. The offense is now balanced and in position to run a new play. (See Diagram 2-6.) Player (4) may then pass to either wing and the motion would be repeated. See Diagrams 2-7, 2-8, and 2-9.

As shown in Diagrams 2-7 through 2-9, (4) chose to key Play #1 again.

Play #2—Screen-the-Wing Play

This time (1), after passing to wing man (2) as shown in Diagram 2-10, screens away for the offside wing man (3), who cuts to the point. This tells the onside post man (4) to screen away for the offside post man (5), who cuts to the ballside high post area.

Player (1) then cuts off (4) to the ballside low post area. See Diagram 2-11.

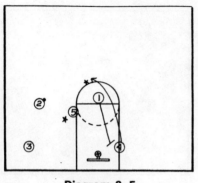

Diagram 2-5

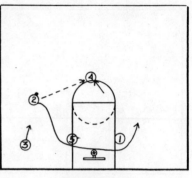

Diagram 2-6

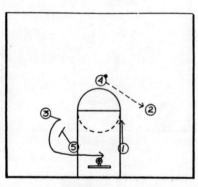

Diagram 2-7

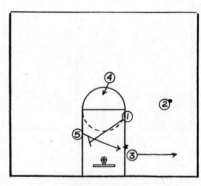

Diagram 2-8

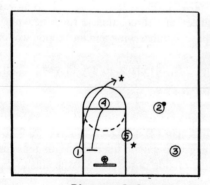

Diagram 2-9

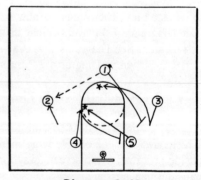

Diagram 2-10

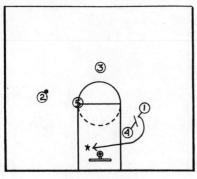

Diagram 2–11

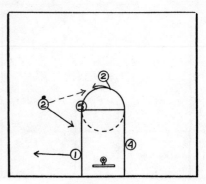

Diagram 2–12

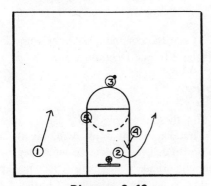

Diagram 2–13

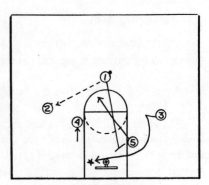

Diagram 2–14

Balancing Move

If (1) is not open, (2) passes to (3) as (1) clears to the corner. See Diagram 2-12. After his pass, (2) clears to the offside wing as (1) moves up to replace (2). See Diagram 2-13.

The offense is now balanced and (3) may pass to either wing and initiate a new sequence of cuts.

Play #3—Quick Downscreen

This time after (1) passes to a wing (as to (2) in Diagram 2-14), he immediately screens down for the offside post man (5). This forms an almost double screen for (3), who cuts to the ballside post area as (5) uses (1)'s screen to cut to the point.

Player (4) then screens away for (1) as (3) clears to the ballside corner; (1) cuts to the ballside post area. See Diagram 2-15.

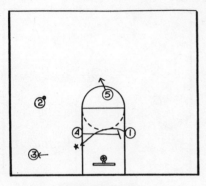

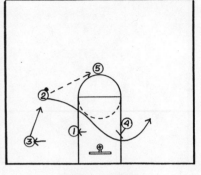

Diagram 2-15   Diagram 2-16

Balancing Move

If (1) is not open, (2) passes to (5) and the continuity is reset with (2) moving to the offside wing and (3) replacing (2). See Diagram 2-16.

Reading and Timing the Basic Motions

In order to differentiate and then time these three plays, the players must key on (1). If (1) chooses to run the wing first play, he passes to a wing (as to (2) in Diagram 2-17) and delays. If (1) chooses to call the screen-the-wing play, he must (after passing) cut directly to screen the offside wing man's defender. See Diagram 2-18. He should have time to do this because (3) is taught to make a change of direction before making any cut. If (1) chooses to run the quick downscreen for the offside post man, he must pass to the wing and immediately screen down as (3) cuts over (5). See Diagram 2-19.

Once one of these keys is established, the resulting continuity motion should flow smoothly.

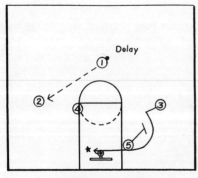

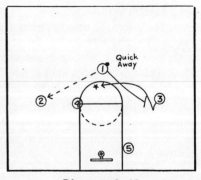

Diagram 2-17   Diagram 2-18

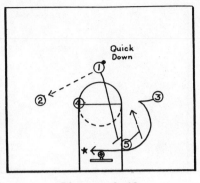

Diagram 2–19

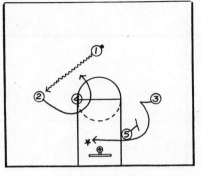

Diagram 2–20

PRESSURE RELIEVERS

The prevalence of pressure-help pass-denying defenses necessitates the use of pressure relievers. The following three options permit the continuity to negate pressure and flow smoothly.

Point-to-Wing Dribble Entry

In Diagram 2-20, point man (1) cannot make an entry pass to either wing to initiate the continuity. He has maintained his dribble and opts to use the dribble entry by dribbling at wing man (2). This tells (2) to loop around the ballside post man and move to the point. It also tells the offside wing man (3) to cut off the offside post man (5).

If (3) is not open, he clears to the ballside corner and the post men (4) and (5) exchange. See Diagram 2-21.

Player (2) then screens down for (4) who pops to the point and receives a pass from (1). See Diagrams 2-22 and 2-23. Players (1) and (3) then balance the offense by moving to the wings, and the next sequence may be initiated by the new point man (4). See Diagram 2-24.

Wing-to-Point Denial Option

This time, the cuts have been made and the feeder at the wing (2) cannot pass to the point to allow another sequence to be run. He overcomes this denial by dribbling at the man at the point ((4) in Diagram 2-25) and clearing him to the far wing position.

From there (2) can pass to either wing (as to (4) in Diagram 2-26) and initiate a new play.

In the above play, (2) chose to call Play #2—the screen-the-wing play.

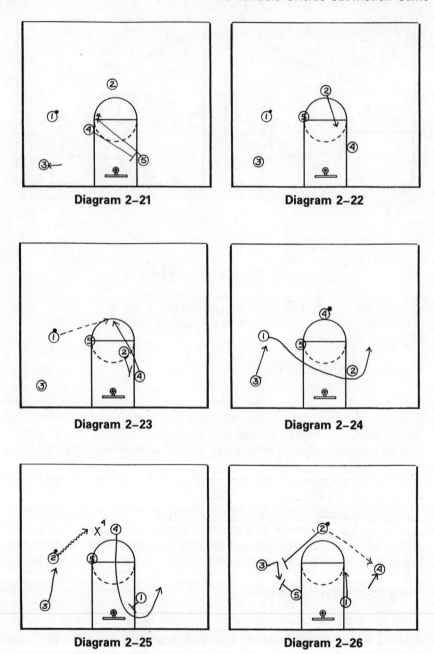

Diagram 2-21

Diagram 2-22

Diagram 2-23

Diagram 2-24

Diagram 2-25

Diagram 2-26

Balancing Move Denial

At times, when the pass to the point that initiates the balancing move is being denied, the following option may be keyed. In Diagram 2-27, (2) is unable to pass to either the post man (5) or the point man (1). When this occurs, he may pass to (3) in the corner and clear to the offside wing. Player (3) then dribbles to the wing as (1) changes direction to get open.

From there, (1) may initiate the next motion sequence.

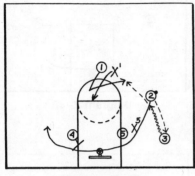 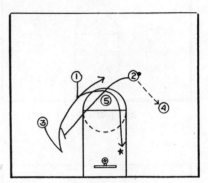

Diagram 2–27   **Diagram 2–28**

AUXILIARY PLAYS

The following plays may be used to give the offense depth or to take advantage of specific team strengths or opposition weaknesses in a particular game.

Two-Man Front Play

This play is designed for the team that lacks a dominant guard who can control the ball versus pressure until a play can be initiated.

In Diagram 2-28, the two guards (1) and (2) bring the ball upcourt and (2) initiates a play by passing to his forward (4) and crossing to screen away for forward (3) who moves to the point. Guard (1) utilizes (2)'s crossing action and cuts to the ballside low post area for a possible lay-up pass.

If (1) is not open, the ball is then reversed to (2) by way of (3). Player (5) then swings to (2)'s side. See Diagram 2-29.

Player (3) may then: (A) delay and call the wing first play (Diagram 2-30), (B) quickly screen away and call the screen-away play (Diagram 2-31), or (C) quickly screen down and call the quick downscreen play (Diagram 2-32).

UCLA Slash Play

The UCLA Slash Play may be used as an entry to this continuity.

Diagram 2-33 shows (1) passing to wing man (2) and making his slash cut off high post man (4). If (1) is not open, he clears to the ballside corner. Note that (3) replaced (1) at the point.

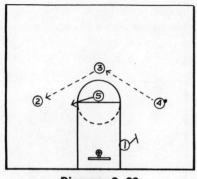

Diagram 2-29

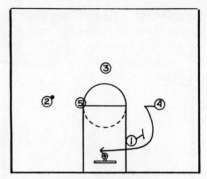

Diagram 2-30

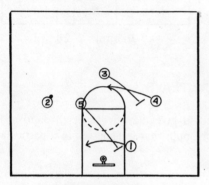

Diagram 2-31

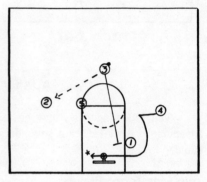

Diagram 2-32

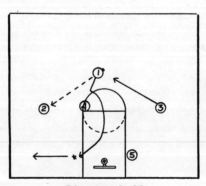

Diagram 2-33

This slash cut replaces the cut by the offside wing and is followed by a post exchange with (4) screening for the offside post man who cuts to the ballside post area. See Diagram 2-34. Player (3) then screens down for (4) who pops to the point. See Diagram 2-35.

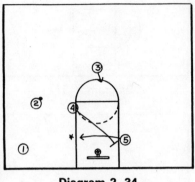

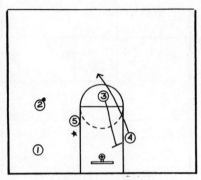

Diagram 2–34   **Diagram 2–35**

Balancing Move

If (2) passes to (4), he moves to the offside wing area (1) and replaces him. See Diagram 2-36. The team is then in position to run the basic continuity. See Diagram 2-37.

Dribble Entry #1 Play

One dribble entry to the basic continuity begins as (1) dribbles at (2) and clears him to the ballside corner. This tells the onside post man ((4) in Diagram 2-38) to move high and the offside wing man (3) to cut off the offside low post man (5). Player (4) then screens away for (5) who cuts to the point. See Diagram 2-39.

Balancing Move

Player (1) then passes to (5) and clears to the offside wing area as (2) replaces him. See Diagram 2-40. Player (5) then passes to a wing as to (1) in Diagram 2-41 and the continuity goes on.

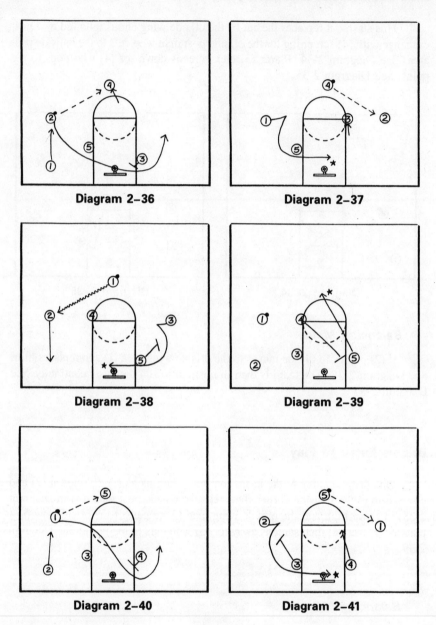

Diagram 2–36

Diagram 2–37

Diagram 2–38

Diagram 2–39

Diagram 2–40

Diagram 2–41

Dribble Entry #2 Play

Another dribble entry that might be considered is as follows. Player (1) dribbles at (2) and clears him down and across the lane. This tells the onside post man (4) to screen high and away for (3) who cuts over him looking for a pass from (1). See Diagrams 2-42 and 2-43.

If (1) cannot pass to (3), (4) pops to the head of the key and receives the pass. Player (2) then moves out of (5)'s downscreen and (4) passes to him. See Diagram 2-44. Player (5) moves high and (1) cuts off (3) to start the basic continuity. See Diagram 2-45.

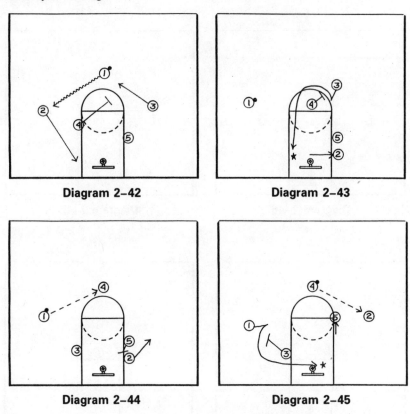

Diagram 2-42   **Diagram 2-43**

Diagram 2-44   **Diagram 2-45**

VERSUS ZONE DEFENSES

With a few simple adaptations, the basic man-to-man continuity can be used as a zone offense.

The Basic Motion

Diagram 2-46 shows (1) passing to wing man (2). This pass usually keys the offside wing man (3) to cut low off post man (5). This time, however, it tells the ballside post man (4) to drop low and the offside wing man (3) to cut to the high post area.

If (2) can then get the ball to (3), a triangle play results; (3) may then shoot or look for (4) and (5) inside the zone. If (2) cannot pass to the middle, (3) clears to the ballside corner to create an overload. See Diagram 2-47.

At that point, the post exchange occurs but with different timing. Player (5) cuts to the high post area; if (2) can pass to him, he, (5), looks inside for (4). See Diagram 2-48. If (2) cannot pass to (5), (4) clears away and (5) drops to the ballside low post area. See Diagram 2-49.

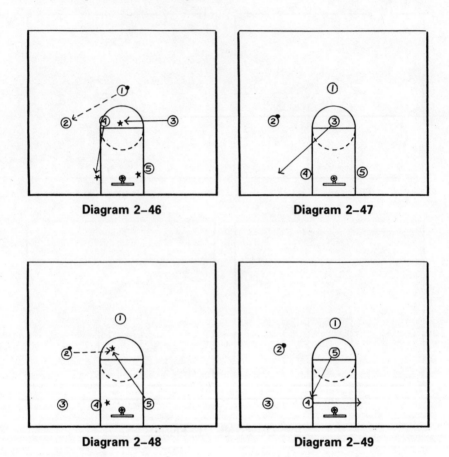

Diagram 2–46   Diagram 2–47

Diagram 2–48   Diagram 2–49

Balancing Move

Players (2), (1), (3), and (5) then utilize the overload until (2) desires to change it. See Diagram 2-50. He does this by passing to (1) and clearing to the offside wing. Player (3) then replaces (2). See Diagrams 2-51 and 2-52.

In Diagram 2-53, (1)'s pass to (2) restarts the continuity and keys (3)'s cut to the high post to form a new triangle play.

This adaptation of the basic continuity has great zone potential because it consists of a triangle play, an overload, and a quick reversal to an overshifted screen. If necessary versus zones, it may be complemented by a version of dribble entry play.

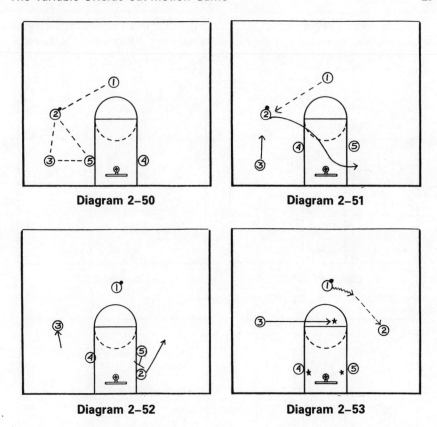

Diagram 2–50 Diagram 2–51

Diagram 2–52 Diagram 2–53

Dribble Entry Play

Player (1) dribbles at (2) and clears him to the ballside corner; (3) then replaces (1) at the point. Diagram 2-54 shows the resulting overload. Players (1), (2), (3), and (4) then utilize this overload by moving the ball. The post men make their exchange as the ball is being passed around the overload. See Diagrams 2-55 and 2-56.

Balancing Move

Wing man (1) may change the overload when he chooses by passing to (3) and clearing to the offside wing area. Player (2) would then replace (1). See Diagram 2-57.

From there, (3) may initiate the basic play (Diagram 2-58) or repeat the dribble entry play (Diagram 2-59).

Using the basic man-to-man offense and dribble entry play as a zone offense has distinct advantages. It tests zones in their most vulnerable areas—the corner and middle—and simplifies the coach's job.

    This motion offense is very difficult to defense. It is virtually impossible to
anticipate your man's cut and the motion negates any offside help. The fact that
with a few simple adjustments the offense may be used against zones adds to its
value.

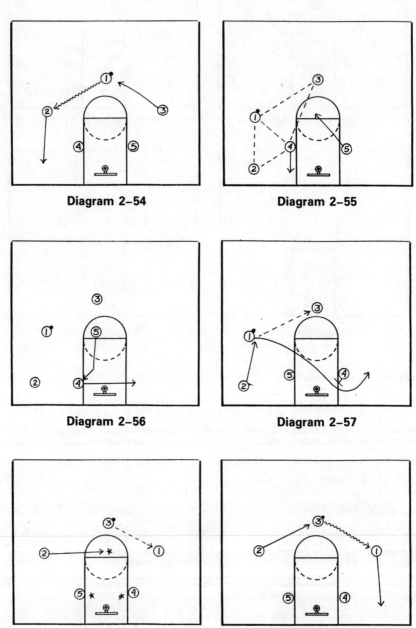

Diagram 2–54   Diagram 2–55

Diagram 2–56   Diagram 2–57

Diagram 2–58   Diagram 2–59

CHAPTER **3**

The
Flex-Plus
Motion

The Flex-Plus Motion is an extension of the very popular Flex Offense. It has all the attributes of the flex, and adds a lob pass option and a double screen option.

PERSONNEL ALIGNMENT

This offense is a five-man motion that works well for teams that lack a post man. Players (1) and (2) are the guards who bring the ball upcourt and initiate the plays. Player (1) should be the taller of the two because he will receive most of the lob passes; (5) is the high post man who attempts to set up on the ballside; (3) and (4) are the forwards who need adequate overall skills, but may be small in stature. In general, this offense is designed for five mobile players who can operate within the context of motion. See Diagram 3-1.

THE BASIC MOTION

The Flex

As previously stated, this motion is an offshoot of the Flex Continuity Offense. The flex is a five-man motion with two basic options. As shown in Diagram 3-2, it begins as (1) makes a guard-to-guard pass to (2). This pass keys the offside forward (3) to cut off post man (5) and move to the basket. Player (1) then screens down for (5) who moves to the guard position. See Diagram 3-3.

After (2) passes to (5), the same two options are repeated with (3) screening for (4) and (2) screening down for (3). See Diagram 3-4.

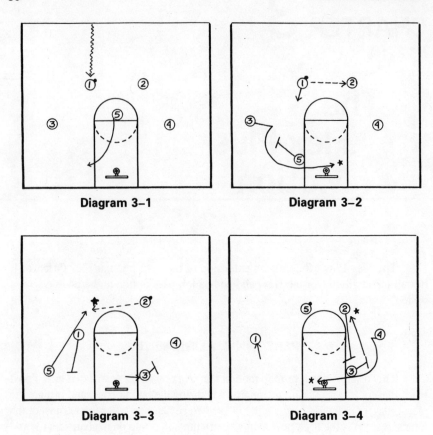

Diagram 3–1   Diagram 3–2

Diagram 3–3   Diagram 3–4

The Flex-Plus

The Flex-Plus Offense begins with (5) in a high post position on the ballside. After the guard-to-guard pass is made (as from (1) to (2) in Diagram 3-5), (1) cuts off post man (5) to the offside lay-up slot for a possible lob pass.

If (1) is not open, (2) passes to the forward on his side, (4). This keys (3) to cut off (1) to the ballside low post area. See Diagram 3-6.

If (3) is open as he moves under the basket, (4) should pass to him. If (3) is not open, (2) and (5) screen down and away for (1), who cuts to the ballside head of the key. See Diagram 3-7.

Player (4) then passes to (1) who may shoot or run the motion again by passing to (2). Player (2), who was the inside man on the double screen, loops around (5) and to a guard position; (5) moves to the free throw line extended. Also note that on the pass from (4) to (1), (3) moved up to the high post position. See Diagram 3-8.

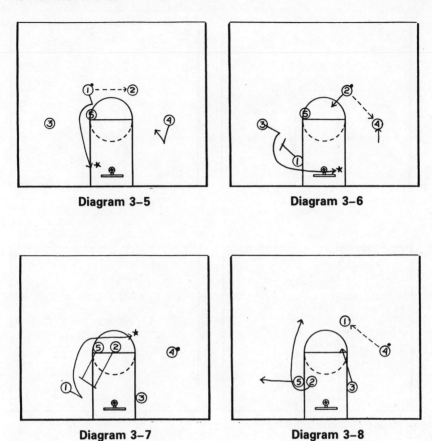

Diagram 3-5

Diagram 3-6

Diagram 3-7

Diagram 3-8

Once (1) passed to (2), the pattern would again consist of: (A) a lob pass to (1), keyed by (1)'s pass to (2) (Diagram 3-9), (B) the offside cut of (4) off (1), keyed by (2)'s pass to (5) (Diagram 3-10), (C) the double screen down and away by (2) and (3) (Diagram 3-11), and (D) the reset phase with (2) looping around (3) to a guard position, and (3) moving wide (Diagram 3-12).

Shuffle Cut Option

The Shuffle Cut Option converts the Flex-Plus Motion into a five-man interchangeable motion.

At the point of the guard-to-forward pass ((2) to (4) as shown in Diagram 3-13), the passing guard and the high post man usually screen away for the offside screener (1).

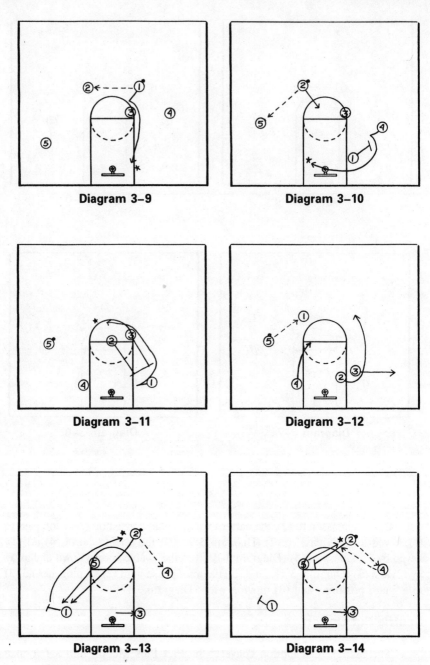

Diagram 3–9

Diagram 3–10

Diagram 3–11

Diagram 3–12

Diagram 3–13

Diagram 3–14

When using the Shuffle Cut Option, (2) comes down and screens for high post man (5) who pops to the ballside point. See Diagram 3-14. Player (2) then continues his cut and screens for (1), who cuts to the offside guard position. See Diagram 3-15.

From there, (5) passes to (1), cuts off (3) (who moved to the high post area) for a possible lob pass. The same motion is then repeated. See Diagrams 3-16 through 3-18.

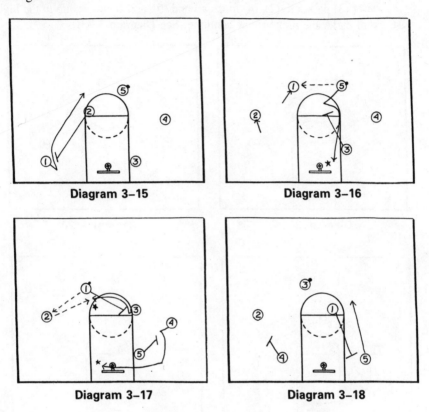

Diagram 3–15   Diagram 3–16

Diagram 3–17   Diagram 3–18

PRESSURE RELIEVERS

Guard-to-Guard Pass Denial

When the guard-to-guard pass is being denied, the simplest remedy is a guard-to-forward exchange ((2) to (4)) as shown in Diagram 3-19.

Dribble Entry

This play too may be used when the guard-to-guard pass is being denied. It may also be used as an entry into the motion that adds variety.

Diagram 3-20 shows the pass from (1) to (2) being denied. Seeing this, (1) dribbles at (3) and clears him across the lane to the far wing area. Player (2) reads this key and cuts over post man (5) looking for a pass from (1).

If (2) is not open, (1) passes to (4) at the point, who reverses it to (3). Player (1) then cuts off (2) and moves to the ballside low post area. See Diagram 3-21. Players (4) and (5) then double screen down and away for (2). See Diagram 3-22.

Player (3) passes to (2), (4) loops around (5), and (1) moves up to the high post. From there, the motion may continue. See Diagram 3-23.

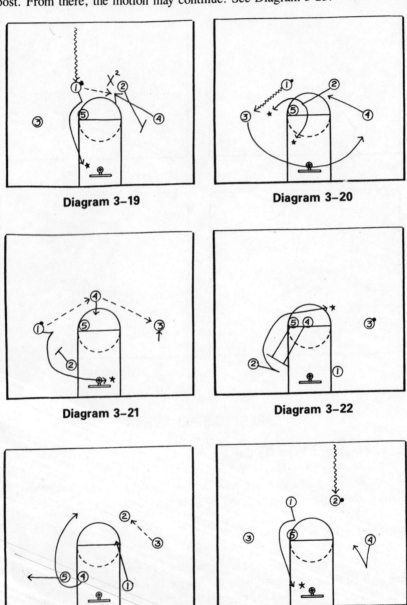

Diagram 3-19

Diagram 3-20

Diagram 3-21

Diagram 3-22

Diagram 3-23

Diagram 3-24

From there, (5) passes to (1), cuts off (3) (who moved to the high post area) for a possible lob pass. The same motion is then repeated. See Diagrams 3-16 through 3-18.

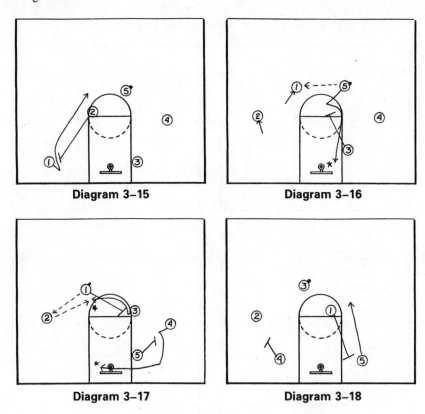

Diagram 3–15	Diagram 3–16
Diagram 3–17	Diagram 3–18

PRESSURE RELIEVERS

Guard-to-Guard Pass Denial

When the guard-to-guard pass is being denied, the simplest remedy is a guard-to-forward exchange ((2) to (4)) as shown in Diagram 3-19.

Dribble Entry

This play too may be used when the guard-to-guard pass is being denied. It may also be used as an entry into the motion that adds variety.

Diagram 3-20 shows the pass from (1) to (2) being denied. Seeing this, (1) dribbles at (3) and clears him across the lane to the far wing area. Player (2) reads this key and cuts over post man (5) looking for a pass from (1).

If (2) is not open, (1) passes to (4) at the point, who reverses it to (3). Player (1) then cuts off (2) and moves to the ballside low post area. See Diagram 3-21. Players (4) and (5) then double screen down and away for (2). See Diagram 3-22.

Player (3) passes to (2), (4) loops around (5), and (1) moves up to the high post. From there, the motion may continue. See Diagram 3-23.

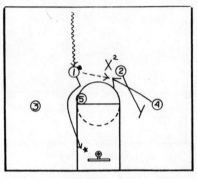

Diagram 3–19

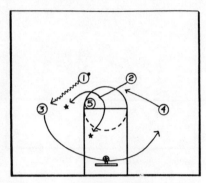

Diagram 3–20

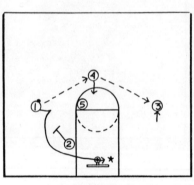

Diagram 3–21

Diagram 3–22

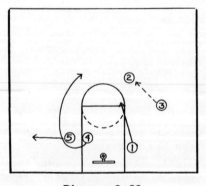

Diagram 3–23

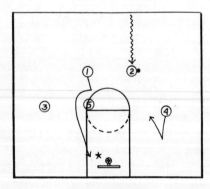

Diagram 3–24

Weakside Entry

In the event the ball is brought upcourt on the weakside and (5) does not adjust to that side, the basic motion is timed as follows: As the dribbling guard on the weakside ((2) in Diagram 3-24) picks up his dribble, guard (1) cuts off the high post.

If (1) is not open, (2) passes to (4) to key the offside cut followed by the offside downscreen by (2) and (5). See Diagrams 3-25 and 3-26.

Player (4) passes to (1) and the pattern is reset with (2) looping out front and (5) moving wide, and (3) moving up to the high post. See Diagram 3-27.

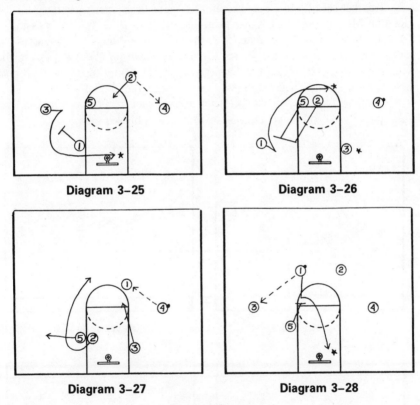

Diagram 3-25   Diagram 3-26

Diagram 3-27   Diagram 3-28

AUXILIARY PLAYS

Many of the popular set plays in use today may be used as entry vehicles to the basic Flex-Plus Motion. Some of these plays are:

De Paul Cut

Diagram 3-28 shows guard (1) passing to forward (3) and cutting off high post man (5) to the offside post area for a possible lob pass.

As soon as the possibility for the lob pass is over and (1) assumes a screening position, (4) cuts off (1) to the ballside post area. See Diagram 3-29.

After (4)'s cut, (2) and (5) screen down for (1), who moves to the ballside head of the key. See Diagram 3-30.

Player (3) passes to (1), (5) loops to a guard position, (2) moves out wide and (4) assumes a high post position. From there, the basic motion may be continued. See Diagram 3-31.

UCLA Slash Cut Play

Another set play that may be run to provide the proper pattern set for the Flex-Plus Motion is the UCLA Slash Cut Play. Diagram 3-32 shows (1) passing to (3) and cutting off high post man (5) to the ballside post area; (5) then steps out and receives a pass from (3). Player (3) screens down for (1), who pops to the wing position. After setting the downscreen for (1), (3) moves to the high post area; (2) and (4) exchange on the offside. See Diagram 3-33.

Player (5) may now pass to (1) for a jump shot or, as shown in Diagram 3-34, pass to (4) and make a cut off (3) for a possible lob pass.

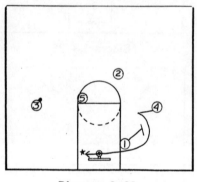

Diagram 3–29

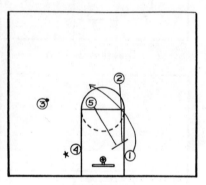

Diagram 3–30

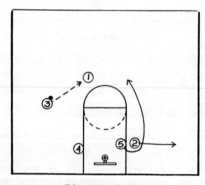

Diagram 3–31

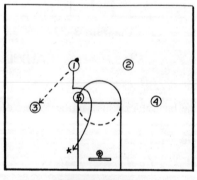

Diagram 3–32

From there, the basic Flex-Plus Motion options will follow. See Diagrams 3-35, 3-36, and 3-37.

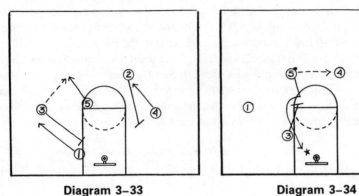

Diagram 3–33   **Diagram 3–34**

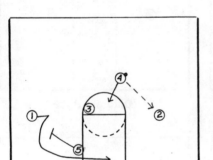
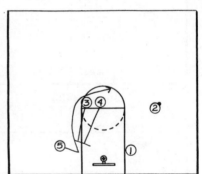

Diagram 3–35   **Diagram 3–36**

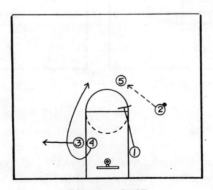

Diagram 3–37

Shuffle Cross Play

This entry maneuver is a popular pattern set play for shuffle teams. Diagram 3-38 shows (1) passing to forward (3) and making a cut over post man (5), to form a natural screen for (2), to cut to the ballside post area. The offside forward (4) uses (1) as a natural screen and cuts to the point.

Player (3) looks first for (2) and, if he is not open, passes to (4) at the point; (5) moves to the offside and stacks with (1). See Diagram 3-39.

Player (1) uses (5)'s downscreen to move to a guard position. Also note that (3)'s pass to (4) keyed (2) to move to the high post. See Diagram 3-40. The basic motion follows with (4) passing to (1) as the key. See Diagram 3-41.

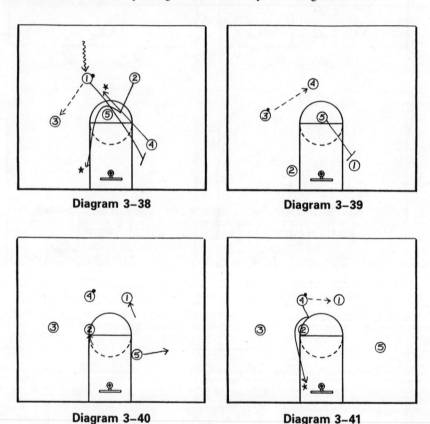

Diagram 3-38   Diagram 3-39

Diagram 3-40   Diagram 3-41

Cross-the-Lane Play

This time, after (1) passes to (2) and cuts off high post man (5), he moves across the lane to the ballside low post area. See Diagram 3-42. From there, two options are available:

Strongside Option

Player (2) quickly passes to (4), and (2) and (5) screen away for (3), who moves to the ballside head of the key. See Diagram 3-43. The offense is then reset. See Diagram 3-44.

Note in Diagram 3-43 that (3) faked a cut across the lane before moving out front.

Weakside Option

This time (2), after receiving the pass from (1), dribbles toward (3) on the weakside and passes to him. See Diagrams 3-45 and 3-46. This maneuver tells (4) to cut off (1) and move to the ballside post area. See Diagram 3-47.

Players (2) and (5) then screen down for (1), who pops to the ballside head of the key. See Diagram 3-48.

Then (3) passes to (1), (4) moves up to the high post, (5) loops around (2) and out to a guard position, (2) moves wide, and the team is in position to run another Flex-Plus sequence. See Diagram 3-49.

Note: This Cross-the-Lane Play may also be initiated with (1) passing to (2) and making a shuffle out across the lane. See Diagram 3-50.

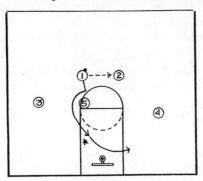

Diagram 3-42

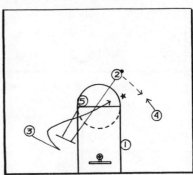

Diagram 3-43

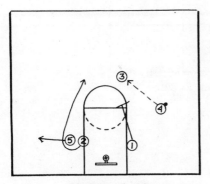

Diagram 3-44

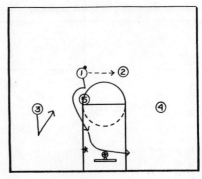

Diagram 3-45

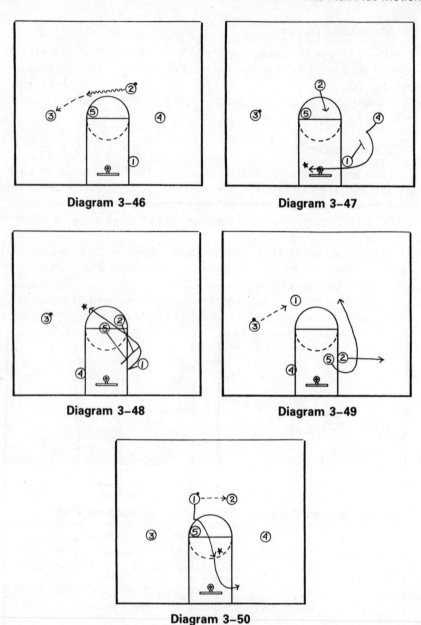

Diagram 3–46   Diagram 3–47

Diagram 3–48   Diagram 3–49

Diagram 3–50

Post-to-Point Play

This play is a variation of the basic Flex-Plus Motion. It begins as shown in Diagram 3-51 with guard (1) passing to guard (2) and cutting off high post man (5) to the offside lay-up slot for a possible lob pass.

Player (5) keys the post-to-point play by moving out front; (2) fakes to (5) and passes to (4). This pass tells (3) to make his offside cut. This time, however, (3) fakes a cut below (1) and cuts to the high post area. See Diagram 3-52.

If (3) receives a pass from (4), he may shoot, or look for (1) posting up inside. If (3) does not receive a pass, he continues his cut to the ballside high post area. See Diagram 3-53.

As soon as (3) is across the lane, (2) cuts down the lane. Then (1) screens down for (2) and the ball is reversed to him by way of (5). See Diagrams 3-54 and 3-55.

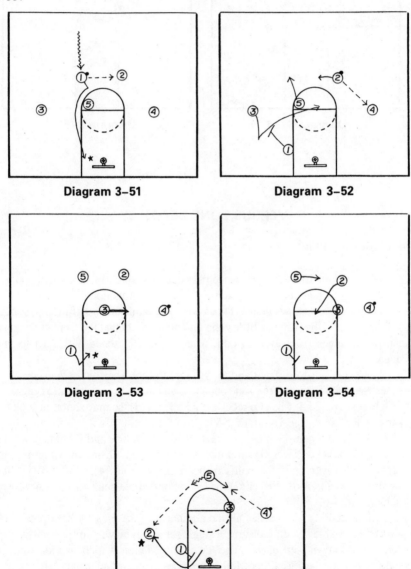

Diagram 3–51   **Diagram 3–52**

Diagram 3–53   **Diagram 3–54**

Diagram 3–55

The motion is then reset. Player (2) keys this by dribbling out front. This tells (5) to cut off (3) and restart the post-to-point motion. See Diagrams 3-56 and 3-57.

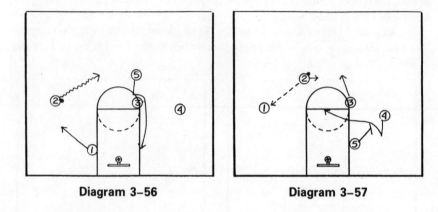

Diagram 3–56   Diagram 3–57

VERSUS ZONE DEFENSES

Post-to-Point Play

If you decide to use the offensive plan in this chapter, I suggest that you use the post-to-point play as a zone offense. It is a very functional zone plan.

Diagram 3-58 shows guard (1) passing to (2) and cutting off high post man (5). This phase of the play has little zone potential except that the front of the zone perimeter changes from even to odd. Many matching zones will react to this change.

Player (5) steps out front and the front of the zone perimeter is even again; (2) then fakes to (5) to pull the zone out and then passes to (4). Player (3) cuts into the high post area and if he can receive a pass from (4), he may shoot, or look for (1) inside the zone. See Diagram 3-59.

If (3) is not open, he moves to the ballside of the lane and (2) cuts down the lane and around (1). Player (1) attempts to trap the zone inside by screening the nearest zone player until the ball can be reversed from (4) to (5) to (1). See Diagrams 3-60 and 3-61. Player (2) may shoot or dribble out front for a new play. See Diagram 3-62.

The Flex-Plus Motion has all the attributes of the Flex Offense plus a lob option and a double screen replacing a single screen. It may be initiated by way of several well-known set plays. The Post-Out Motion which works well in conjunction with the Flex-Plus Motion provides an excellent zone plan.

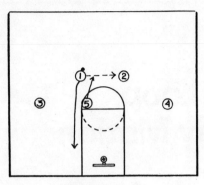

Diagram 3-58

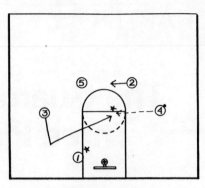

Diagram 3-59

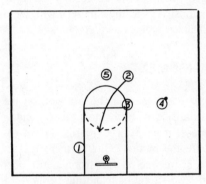

Diagram 3-60

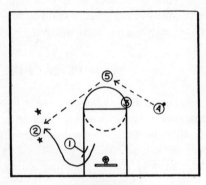

Diagram 3-61

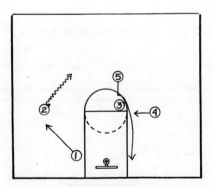

Diagram 3-62

CHAPTER 4

The Guard Loop
Three-Play Motion

This offense is a very simple basic plan. However, it may be used successfully at any level of competition. It consists of a single pattern with three options and may be used with very few changes against zone defenses.

PERSONNEL ALIGNMENT

The motion is begun from a two-guard set and may be initiated on the strongside or weakside. The strongside is the side with the most players and is usually determined by the location of the post man (5). The guards (1) and (2) must be able to resist pressure and initiate the motion. One of them ((2) in Diagram 4-1) should have the ability to score one-on-one from a low post position. The forwards (3) and (4) should have strong ballhandling skills. Post man (5) should have adequate one-on-one skills, be a good passer, and a strong rebounder.

THE BASIC STRONGSIDE MOTION

As shown in Diagram 4-2, (1) passes to his forward (3) and cuts through in a looping manner, down and around the offside forward (4).

From there, the three options are: the split, the reverse, and the high to low post play.

Split Option

After (1) passes to (3) and cuts through, (3) passes to (5) and splits the post with (2). He does this by setting a definite screen for (2), who moves to the ball, and then rolling down the middle. The offside defenders are kept fairly busy handling (4)'s downscreen for (1). See Diagram 4-3.

Player (5) may shoot or pass to the open man; (1) is responsible for defensive balance. If no shot is forthcoming, the ball is passed to (1), who has moved out front. From there, one of two things may be planned. The offense may return to a two-man front or continue from a one-man front.

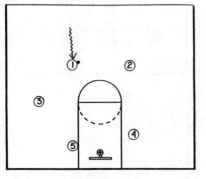

Diagram 4–1

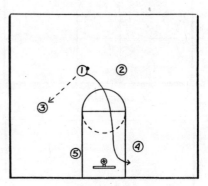

Diagram 4–2

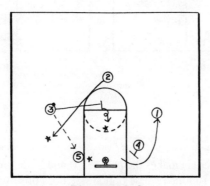

Diagram 4–3

A. Return to a Two-Man Front

Player (1) may dribble away from (2) and bring him out front where the next sequence may be keyed from a two-man front. See Diagrams 4-4 and 4-5.

B. Continue From a One-Man Front

Player (1) may key a new sequence from the one-man front with the offside wing man (2) acting as the second guard. See Diagrams 4-6 and 4-7.

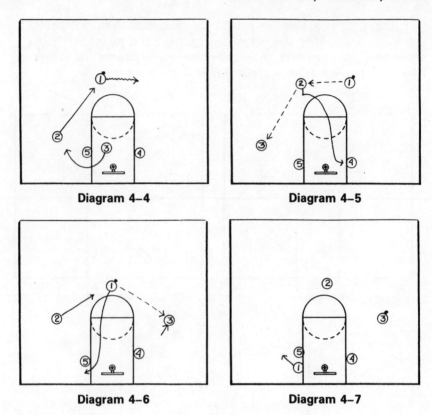

Diagram 4–4   **Diagram 4–5**

Diagram 4–6   **Diagram 4–7**

Reverse Option

This time, after (1) makes the pass to (3) and loops around (4) on the other side, (3) chooses to run the reverse option. He does this by dribbling toward (2) and passing to him. This dribble sets up (3)'s defender (X3) for a screen by (5). See Diagrams 4-8 and 4-9.

Player (2) may then pass to (1) looping around (4), or to (3) cutting off (5)'s screen for a possible lob pass. See Diagram 4-10.

If nothing develops, (2) may initiate a new sequence from this 1-2-2 set with the offside wing man ((3) in Diagram 4-11), acting as the second guard. If you prefer to run each sequence from the 2-3 set, (2) may dribble away from (1) to call him out front and then initiate a new play. See Diagram 4-12.

High to Low Post Option

Player (1) again passes and cuts through and (3) may call a split play by passing to (5), call a reverse by passing to (2), or run the high to low post option. This option is actually called by the offside inside man ((4) in Diagram 4-13); (4) observes that post man (5) is being fronted. This tells (4) to pop to the high post

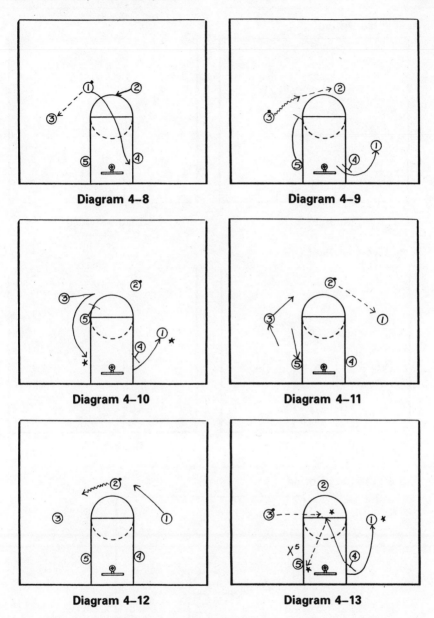

Diagram 4–8

Diagram 4–9

Diagram 4–10

Diagram 4–11

Diagram 4–12

Diagram 4–13

area and receive a pass from (3). He then looks for (5), who boxes out his defender and receives a pass for a power lay-up shot.

Player (1) again maintains defensive balance. If a shot is not available, the ball is passed outside and the pattern is reset in a 2-3 or 1-2-2 set.

Diagrams 4-14 through 4-18 show the offense being run as a continuous motion and using all three options.

It might be wise to run these three options in various orders as a shadow drill in practice with a shot taken on the completion of the third option.

A. Reverse Option

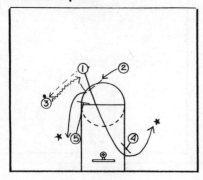

Diagram 4–14

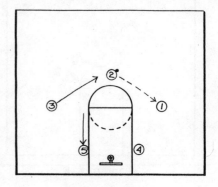

Diagram 4–15

B. High to Low Post Option

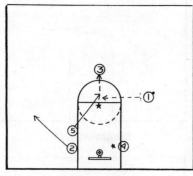

Diagram 4–16

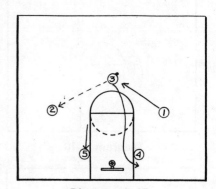

Diagram 4–17

C. Split the Post Option

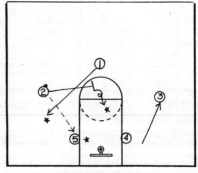

Diagram 4–18

THE BASIC WEAKSIDE MOTION

The weakside motion begins on the side opposite the post man. In Diagram 4-19 post man (5) sets up on (4)'s side and (1) starts the play by passing to (3) and cutting down and around (5) and (4). Player (2) uses (1)'s cut to move toward the ballside.

Post man (5) then uses (1)'s diagonal cut to move to the ballside post area. From there, one of the three basic options may be run. See Diagrams 4-20 through 4-25.

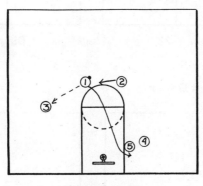

Diagram 4–19

A. Split Option

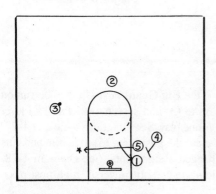

Diagram 4–20

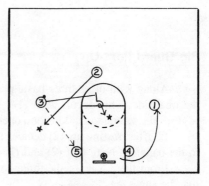

Diagram 4–21

B. Reverse Option

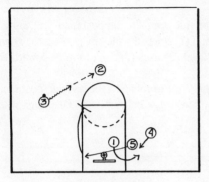

Diagram 4–22

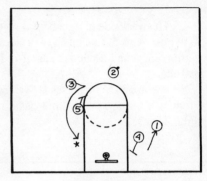

Diagram 4–23

C. High to Low Post Option

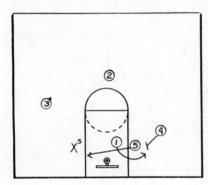

Diagram 4–24

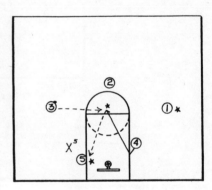

Diagram 4–25

Big Guard Post-Up

Along with these three basic plays, the Big Guard Post-Up may be run on the weakside. This occurs after (1)'s pass to (3) and screen away for (2). Player (2) uses the screen to cut low for a one-on-one play. See Diagrams 4-26 and 4-27.

If, after posting up, (2) decides to clear the post area, (5) uses him and cuts to the ballside. Note that (2) and (1) changed assignments. See Diagram 4-28.

From there, one of the three basic options (split, reverse, high post pass) may be run.

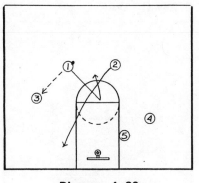

Diagram 4–26

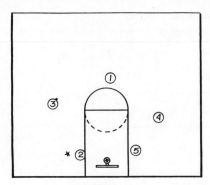

Diagram 4–27

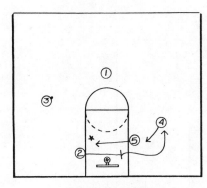

Diagram 4–28

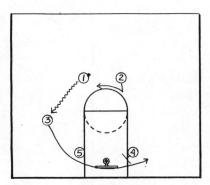

Diagram 4–29

PRESSURE RELIEVERS

The following pressure-relieving plays may be run versus teams that deny the various passes that compose the pattern.

Dribble Entry

In Diagram 4-29, X3 has denied the pass from (1) to (3). Player (1) dribbles at (3) and clears him across the lane and to the offside wing position. Note that (2) made a change of direction before cutting to the ball.

The three basic options may then be run with (1) and (3) changing assignments. See Diagrams 4-30 through 4-32.

A. Split Option

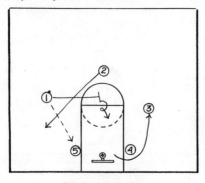

Diagram 4–30

B. Reverse Option

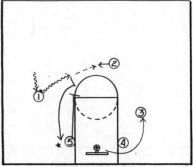

Diagram 4–31

C. High to Low Post Option

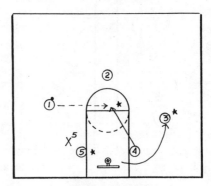

Diagram 4–32

Reversal Denied

When the opposition denies the reversal play, the guard at the point, (2), cuts off forward (4) (who has moved to the high post area), and moves to the offside lay-up area. Player (3) looks for a lob pass to (1). See Diagrams 4-33 and 4-34.

If (2) is not open, he clears to the offside wing, (1) moves to the point, and one of the three basic plays may be run. See Diagram 4-35.

High Post Pass Denial

In Diagram 4-36, X4 denies (3)'s pass to (4) in the high post area. When this happens, (4) makes a change of direction, and cuts to the basket for a lob pass from (3). For this to work, (4) must wait till (1) clears to the wing area. From there, (4) and (1) change jobs and the basic plays may be run.

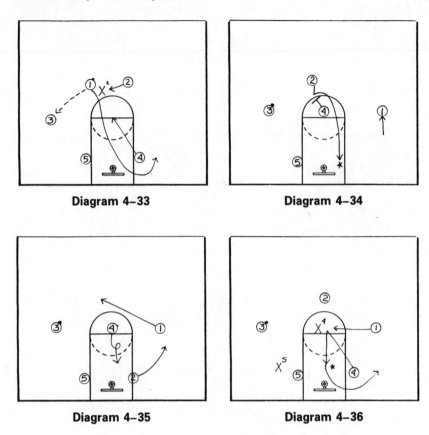

Diagram 4–33   Diagram 4–34

Diagram 4–35   Diagram 4–36

AUXILIARY PLAYS

The following are other plays that may be added as the season progresses.

Backdoor Split Play

In Diagram 4-37 guard (1) comes upcourt and passes directly to (5). This tells (3) to backdoor his overplaying defender and cut to the basket. At the same time, (1) and (2) split the post; (1) cuts first and (2) uses him as a natural screen to cut to the ball. Player (4) steps out and screens for (1), who moves to the offside wing area for a possible jump shot.

Weave Play (A Weakside Play)

In Diagram 4-38 (1) passes to (3) and cuts through; (3) uses (1) as a natural screen and moves toward (2). Player (3) may then hand off to (2) who can possibly go all the way to the basket. See Diagram 4-39.

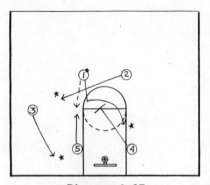

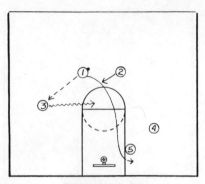

Diagram 4-37   **Diagram 4-38**

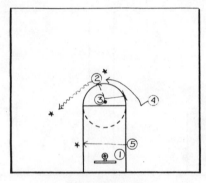

Diagram 4-39

As soon as (2) is stopped, (5) cuts off (1), and (4) cuts off (3). They move to the ball for possible shot options. See Diagram 4-40.

From there, one of the three plays may be run. See Diagrams 4-41 through 4-43.

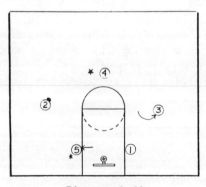

Diagram 4-40

A. Split Option

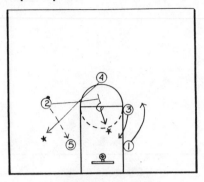

Diagram 4-41

B. Reverse Option

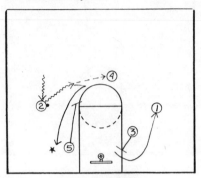

Diagram 4-42

C. High to Low Post Option

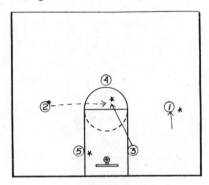

Diagram 4-43

VERSUS ZONE DEFENSES

When playing against zone defenses, the same pattern may be run. Each of the three basic options has a viable function against zone defenses.

Split Option

In Diagrams 4-44 through 4-46, (1) passes to (3) and cuts through. This changes the offensive front from even to odd. Player (3) then passes to (5) and the defense collapses on (5); (3) screens and attempts to trap the zone inside as (2) cuts to the ballside. Note that (1) established defensive balance.

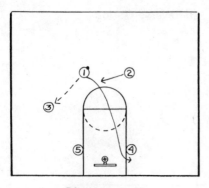

Diagram 4–44

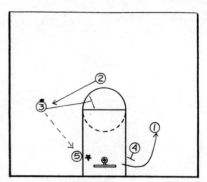

Diagram 4–45

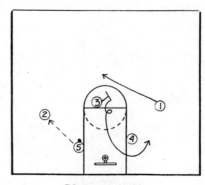

Diagram 4–46

Reverse Option

This time after (1) passes to (3) and cuts through, (3) attempts to reverse the ball to him by way of (2). Player (4) tries to trap the zone inside and allow (1) an easy jump shot. See Diagram 4-47.

High to Low Post Pass Option

Player (1) passes to (3) and makes his cut; (4) cuts high and (3) passes to him. This tells (5) to post up and (1) to backdoor. See Diagrams 4-48 and 4-49.

Player (4) should turn and look for the shot. If the middle man of the zone moves up, (5) may be open. In most cases, (1) will have an open shot. When (3) had the ball, the zone shifted that way. It would be very difficult for the zone to shift back to cover (1).

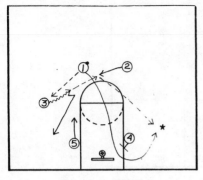

Diagram 4–47

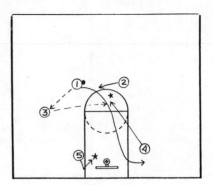

Diagram 4–48

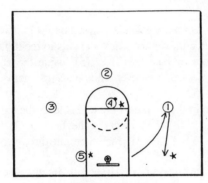

Diagram 4–49

Weakside Zone Action

When the three basic options are run on the weakside, they have the same attributes plus some further advantages versus zones.

Post Across

When the post man breaks to the ballside versus zones, he breaks to an open shot. This pass, if completed, gets the ball inside the zone and leads to many possible options. See Diagram 4-50.

Player (5) may shoot, hit (4) inside the zone, or reverse the ball to (1) at the offside wing.

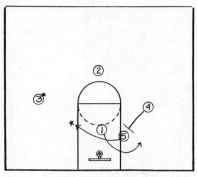

Diagram 4–50

Big Guard Post-Up Play

As per the man-to-man weakside plays, guard (2) may cut to the ballside post area. When this occurs versus zones, (4) cuts to the high post, (3) passes to him, and he may shoot or pass to (2) or (5) inside the zone. This is a very difficult situation for zones to cover and leads to many easy baskets. See Diagrams 4-51 and 4-52.

If (4) is not open in the high post area, (2) clears the ballside post area, and (5) cuts to the ballside; (3) then reverses the ball to (2) by way of (1). See Diagrams 4-53 and 4-54. Player (1) may then cut through and key a new play sequence.

This offense is an example of simplicity in the context of a functional pattern. The three basic plays offer a wide variety of play options that will thoroughly test the defense. The offense may be run successfully against man-to-man, zone, and combination defenses.

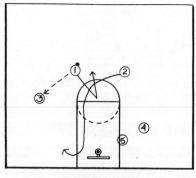

Diagram 4–51

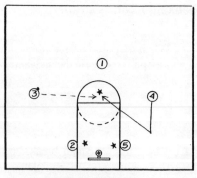

Diagram 4–52

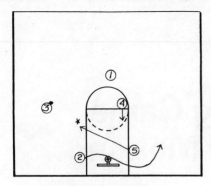

Diagram 4–53

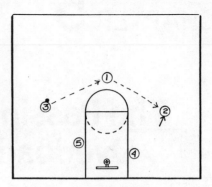

Diagram 4–54

CHAPTER 5

The Passing Game Overload Motion

The Passing Game Overload Motion is versatile in that it may be run as a five-man interchangeable plan, or as an abbreviated continuity that keeps the three small men (1), (2), and (3) on the perimeter, and the two big men (4) and (5) on the inside. It uses the functional pass-and-screen-away maneuver identified with the Passing Game and offers an innovative offensive wrinkle by utilizing an overloaded set. This overload, plus many middle testing cuts, makes it adaptable to zone defenses.

PERSONNEL ALIGNMENT

The motion is begun from a stacked 1-2-2 set. Point man (1) is the team's best ballhandler, players (4) and (5) are the post men and start at the top of the two stacks, and players (2) and (3) are the team's best jump shooters, who need not be very tall. See Diagram 5-1.

THE BASIC MOTION

The basic motion may be initiated from either: (A) a ballside cut overload motion, or (B) an offside cut overload motion.

Ballside Cut Overload Motion

Diagram 5-2 shows point man (1) make a penetrating pass to wing man (2) and cut down the lane to the ballside corner. This motion tells (3) to take the point, and the onside post man (4) to screen away for the offside post man (5), who moves to the ballside post position.

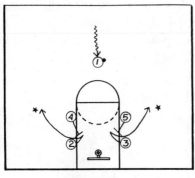
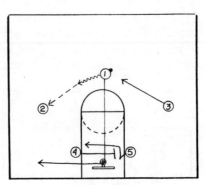

Diagram 5-1   **Diagram 5-2**

The Screen-and-Backdoor Option

At this point, (2) may pass to (5) moving to the ballside and then screen for (1) or (3). The player (either (1) or (3)) who does not receive the screen will backdoor, and the player receiving the screen will utilize it by moving to the ball. Diagram 5-3 shows (2) passing to (5) and screening for (3). This tells (1) to backdoor his defender. After screening, (2) rolls down the middle.

Diagram 5-4 shows (2) passing to (5) and screening for (1). This tells (3) to backdoor his defender. Player (2) again rolls after screening, as (1) utilizes the screen.

In the event (2) cannot pass to (5) to key the screen-and-backdoor option, he passes to (3) moving toward him at the point position. Player (3) reverses the ball to (4), who has moved up to that wing area. Player (2) cuts low off (5), and (1) uses his cut as a natural screen as he makes an arching cut to the high post area. See Diagram 5-5.

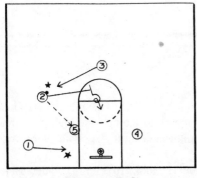
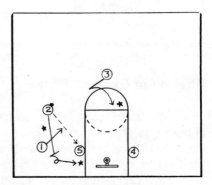

Diagram 5-3   **Diagram 5-4**

If neither (2), nor (1), is open, (2) moves to the ballside corner, and (1) continues his arc to the ballside low post area. See Diagram 5-6.

Player (3) then screens down for (5); (5) uses this screen to move to the point and the motion may be repeated from there. See Diagram 5-7.

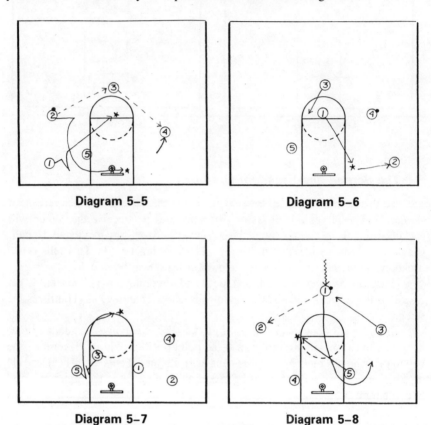

Diagram 5-5   Diagram 5-6

Diagram 5-7   Diagram 5-8

Offside Cut Overload Motion

This time (1) passes to (2) and cuts down the lane to the offside. Post man (5) uses (1)'s cut as a natural screen and moves to the ballside high post area. Player (3) replaces (1) at the point; (1) continues his cut to the offside wing area. See Diagram 5-8.

Player (2), upon receiving the ball from (1), looks first for (4) on the inside. If (4)'s defender (X4) assumes a fronting or strong three-quarter overplay position, (2) may pass to (5) breaking to the high post area. This pass may result in (4)'s being inside his defender and open for a pass from (5) and a power lay-up shot. See Diagram 5-9.

If (2) cannot pass to (4) or (5), (4) clears to the ballside corner and (5) drops low. See Diagram 5-10. From there, (2) may again try to pass to (5) and work a screen-and-backdoor option, or pass to (3), and restart the motion. See Diagram 5-11.

If (1) does not pass to either cutter, (2) moves to the ballside corner and (4) arcs to the low post area. See Diagram 5-12.

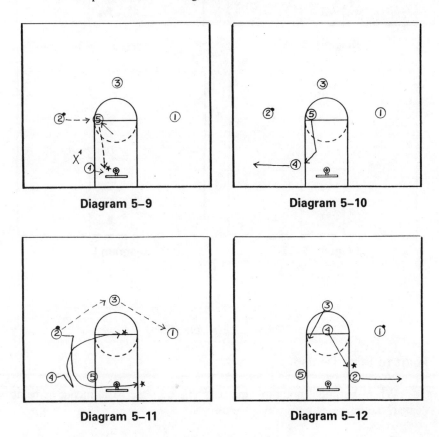

Diagram 5-9   Diagram 5-10

Diagram 5-11   Diagram 5-12

Player (3) screens down for (5), who pops to the point. Player (1) may then pass to (4) and work a screen-and-backdoor option with (5) and (2). See Diagrams 5-13 and 5-14. Or (1) may pass to (5) and restart the continuous motion. See Diagram 5-15.

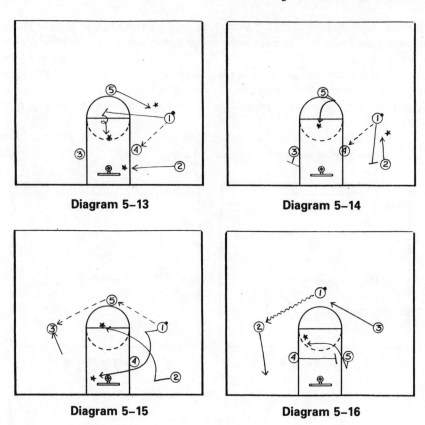

Diagram 5–13   **Diagram 5–14**

Diagram 5–15   **Diagram 5–16**

PRESSURE RELIEVERS

Point to Wing Denied

When the initial point-to-wing pass that keys the basic motion is being denied, the following entries may be utilized.

The Wing-to-Corner Dribble Entry

In Diagram 5-16, point man (1) cannot pass to either wing, so he dribbles at wing man (2) and clears him to the ballside corner. This tells (3) to take the point, and the onside post man (4) to screen away for the offside post man (5) who moves toward the ballside post area.

Player (1) may pass to (5) and work the screen-and-backdoor option, or reverse the ball to (4) by way of (3) to initiate the overload passing game motion. See Diagram 5-17.

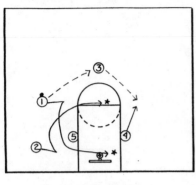

Diagram 5–17

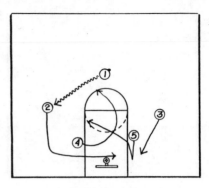

Diagram 5–18

The Wing-Across Dribble Entry

Again, the point-to-wing passes are being denied and (1) dribbles at (2). This time, (2) clears across the lane and (4) pops to the point as (5) moves to the ballside high post area. See Diagram 5-18.

Player (1) reverses the ball to (2) by way of (4); (3) helps (2) get open by screening down for him. See Diagram 5-19. Player (3) posts up and (2) may shoot or pass into (3). Player (5) hesitates and then cuts to the ballside high post area. If (3) is being fronted, a pass from (2) to (5) to (3) may result in a power lay-up shot. See Diagram 5-20.

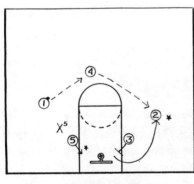

Diagram 5–19

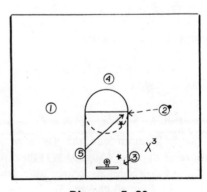

Diagram 5–20

If (2) cannot get the ball to (5), (3) clears to the ballside corner and (4) screens away for (1), who cuts to the point. See Diagram 5-21. Player (2) then passes to (1), who reverses the ball to (4) to start the basic motion. See Diagrams 5-22 and 5-23.

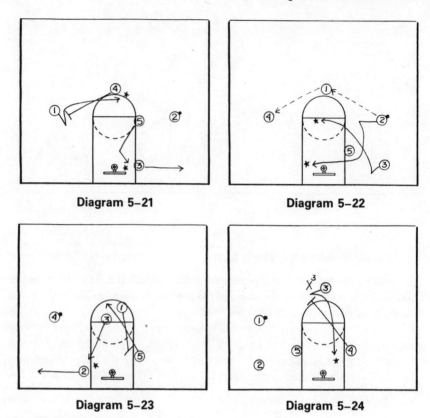

Diagram 5–21   Diagram 5–22

Diagram 5–23   Diagram 5–24

Wing to Point Denied

When the reversal pass from wing to point is being denied, the following options may be run.

Point Lob Option

In Diagram 5-24, the offside wing man (4) notices that (3) is being denied the reversal pass. Wing man (4) then moves up and screens for (3), who cuts off him to the offside lay-up area for a possible lob pass from (1).

If (1) cannot pass to (3), (4) steps to the point and receives a pass from (1). He then reverses it to (3), who has moved to the offside wing area. From there, the basic motion is resumed. See Diagram 5-25.

Wing-to-Point Dribble Clear

A second method to combat the wing-to-point denial is a dribble clear. Seeing that X3 is denying his pass to (3), (1) dribbles at (3) and clears him down the lane and to either corner. In Diagram 5-26, (3) chooses the strongside corner.

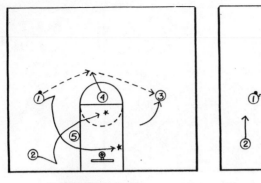

Diagram 5-25

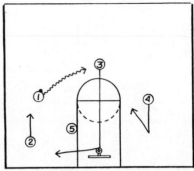

Diagram 5-26

Player (1) passes to (4) moving to the wing and the pattern resumes. See Diagram 5-27.

If (3) chooses to fill the weakside corner, (1) may pass to either wing and the motion will resume at the point of the initial double downscreens. See Diagrams 5-28 through 5-31.

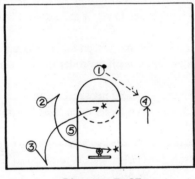

Diagram 5-27

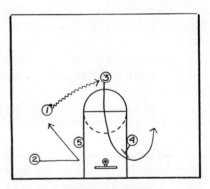

Diagram 5-28

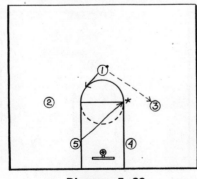

Diagram 5-29

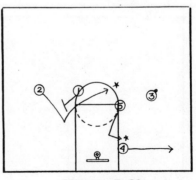

Diagram 5-30

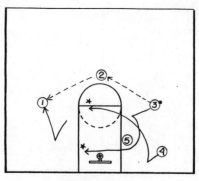

Diagram 5–31

AUXILIARY PLAYS

Corner Play

During the course of the basic motion, a corner play may be inserted. In Diagram 5-32, (4) has the ball at the wing and passes to (1) in the corner. Player (4) cuts through inside (1).

This tells the ballside post man (3) to step out and screen for (1). Player (1) uses the screen by dribbling off it and he may shoot or hit the roller (3) as shown in Diagram 5-33.

If these first two options do not provide a shot, (1) may reverse the ball to (4) by way of (2). Note that (4) used (5)'s downscreen to get open. See Diagram 5-34.

If (4) receives the pass and no shot is open, (3) breaks to the high post, (5) clears to the ballside corner, (2) screens away for (1), the ball is reversed to (2), and the motion is run. See Diagrams 5-35 through 5-37.

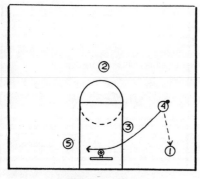

Diagram 5–32

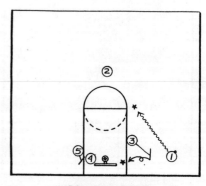

Diagram 5–33

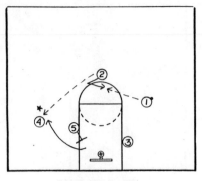

Diagram 5-34

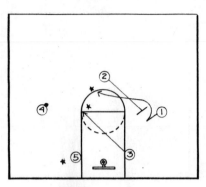

Diagram 5-35

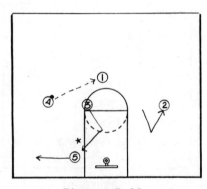

Diagram 5-36

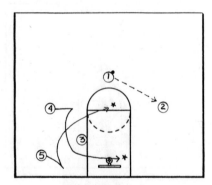

Diagram 5-37

Tight, Inside Motion

When a quick, high percentage shot is desired, the following Tight, Inside Motion may be added. In Diagram 5-38, (1) dribbles at (2) and clears him to the point. This tells the offside wing man (3) to move in tight and screen down for the post man on his side, (5). Player (5) uses this screen as he loops to the ballside high post area.

If (5) receives a pass from (1), he may shoot or look inside for (4). See Diagram 5-39.

If (1) cannot get the ball to (5) or (4), (4) screens away for (3), who cuts to the low post area on the ballside. See Diagram 5-40.

If (3) is not open, (1) passes to (2) at the point. Note that (2) had to make a change of direction to get open. Player (2) then dribbles to the open wing area and the Tight, Inside Motion is repeated. See Diagrams 5-41 through 5-43.

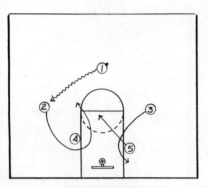

Diagram 5-38

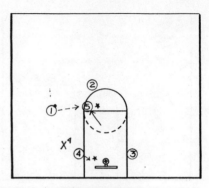

Diagram 5-39

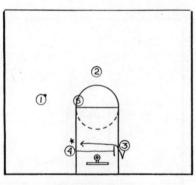

Diagram 5-40

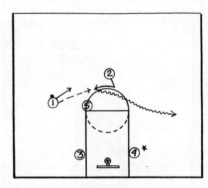

Diagram 5-41

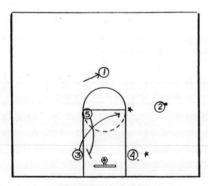

Diagram 5-42

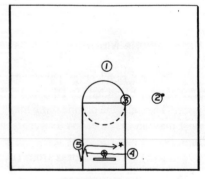

Diagram 5-43

Weakside Entry Play

The Tight, Inside Motion may also be initiated in the following manner. Diagram 5-44 shows point man (2) pass to the weakside wing man (4). This pass tells the strongside wing man ((1) in Diagram 5-45) to cut low off the doublescreen formed by players (5) and (3).

Player (5) screens down for (3), who cuts to the ballside high post area. See Diagram 5-46. Player (1) then screens away for (5), who moves to the ballside low post area. See Diagram 5-47. If nothing develops, (4) passes to (2), and the Tight, Inside Motion is resumed.

This motion works well in conjunction with the Overload Passing Game because it provides a quick, high percentage shot when one is needed.

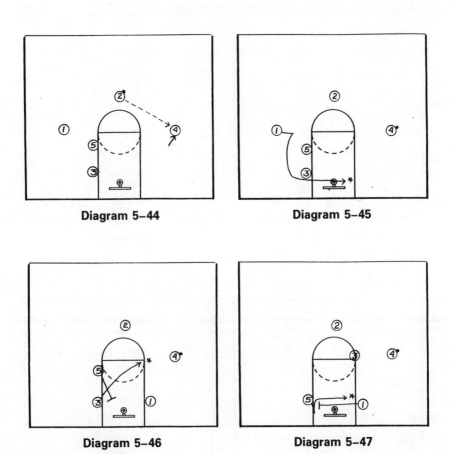

Diagram 5-44   Diagram 5-45

Diagram 5-46   Diagram 5-47

VERSUS ZONE DEFENSES

Ballside Cut Overload Motion

In Diagram 5-48, (1) passes to (2), cuts down the lane, and overloads the ballside by cutting to that corner.

At this point, the timing of the motion is slightly different versus zones. Rather than (4) screening away for (5), as shown in Diagram 5-49, (5) cuts to the high post area on the ballside. If (2) cannot pass to (5), (4) clears across the lane. Player (5) then slides low. See Diagram 5-50.

From there, the overload is maintained and utilized as long as the ball stays on the overloaded side. See Diagram 5-51. Once (3) passes to (4) on the weakside, the motion cuts are made. See Diagram 5-52.

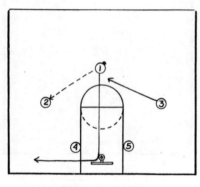

Diagram 5–48

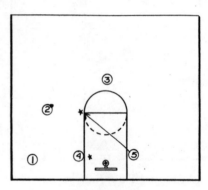

Diagram 5–49

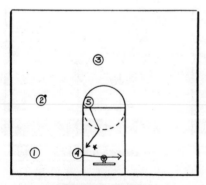

Diagram 5–50

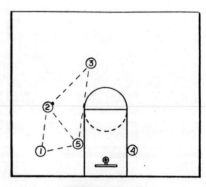

Diagram 5–51

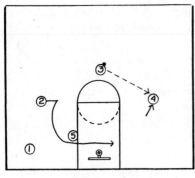

Diagram 5-52

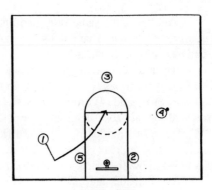

Diagram 5-53

Note that versus zones, the man in the corner ((1) in Diagram 5-53) hesitates and permits (2) to cross the lane before cutting to the high post area.

If (4) can pass to (1), either (5) or (2) may be open inside the zone for a power lay-up shot. See Diagram 5-54.

If (4) cannot pass to (1), (2) clears to the corner and (1) slides to the low post area. From here, the same overload rules and options prevail, with the exception that (3)'s downscreen for (5) is omitted because it has no value versus zones. See Diagram 5-55.

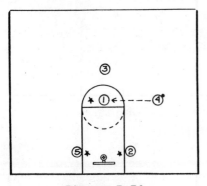

Diagram 5-54

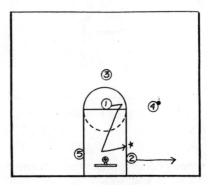

Diagram 5-55

Offside Cut Overload Motion

When (1) passes to (2) and moves down the lane to the offside, (5) cuts off him and to the ballside high post. If (5) receives a pass from (2), he may shoot or look for (4) inside the zone. See Diagram 5-56.

If (2) cannot pass to (5) or (4), (4) clears to the ballside corner to create an overload and (5) drops low. See Diagram 5-57.

From here, the same rules and options prevail as when using the ballside cut overload motion. That entails maintaining the overload until (3) passes to (1). See Diagrams 5-58 and 5-59.

Player (2) cuts across the lane and then (4) cuts high. See Diagram 5-60. Once (2) determines (1) cannot pass to (4) for the triangle play, he clears to the ballside corner and (4) drops low. Note again that (3)'s downscreen for (5) is not executed against zone defenses. See Diagram 5-61.

These two motion plays will suffice as a zone offense. They test the two most vulnerable areas of a zone. Those areas are the corner and high post. The plays also allow the offense to overload and overshift a zone.

The ballside and offside overload passing game motions provide a sweeping type of offense that tends to spread the defense. Most of the shot options are in high percentage areas. The pressure relievers are provided to combat pressure-and-help defenses. The auxiliary plays may be added when and if needed. The fact that this offense may not be used as a zone plan makes it doubly valuable.

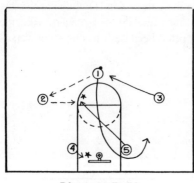

Diagram 5-56

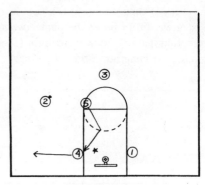

Diagram 5-57

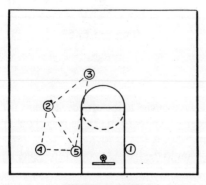

Diagram 5-58

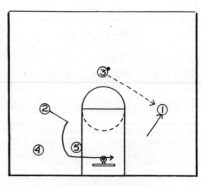

Diagram 5-59

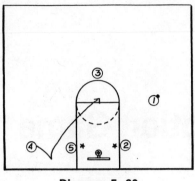

Diagram 5–60   **Diagram 5–61**

CHAPTER 6

The 1-3-1
Wheel Motion Game

The Wheel Motion Game is based on three circular patterns leading to set plays. The Wheel Motion is run until one of the three perimeter players introduces a set play by assuming an overload formation.

PERSONNEL ALIGNMENT

The offense is run from a one-guard ((1)) front, with two wings ((2) and (3)), and a high and low post ((4) and (5)). See Diagram 6-1. It is an abbreviated continuity with (1), (2), and (3) interchanging on the perimeter and big men, (4) and (5), remaining in their area of expertise, the post positions.

THE THREE WHEEL MOTIONS

The three patterns are the slash cut, the lob, and the dribble entry. They are keyed in the following manners:

Slash Cut Key

Player (1) passes to (2), the wing man on the high post man's side, and makes a slash cut off high post man (4), to the ballside lay-up slot. See Diagram 6-2.

Lob Cut Key

This time (1) passes to the wing on the low post man's side, (5), and cuts off (4) to the offside lay-up area for a possible lob pass. See Diagram 6-3.

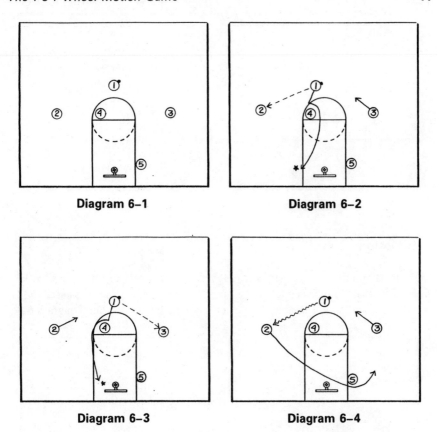

Diagram 6–1   **Diagram 6–2**

Diagram 6–3   **Diagram 6–4**

Dribble Entry Key

Player (1) dribbles at (2) and clears him to the far wing position. See Diagram 6-4.

From there, the three wheel motion patterns operate as follows.

Slash Cut Motion

After (1) passes to (2) and slashes off (4), the offside wing man (3) replaces him at the point. Player (2) passes to (3), who reverses the ball to (1), who has attempted to rub his man off on (5) after cutting across the lane. See Diagrams 6-5 and 6-6.

If (1) had not been open, (3) could have passed to (2) and repeated the slash cut play. Since (3) did pass to (1), it keyed the lob play.

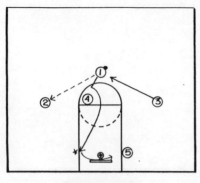
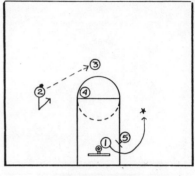

Diagram 6–5   **Diagram 6–6**

Lob Motion

In Diagram 6-7, (3) passed to (1) and then cut off (4) for a possible lob pass. Note that (2) replaced (3) at the point; (3) was not open so (1) passed to (2) at the point and any of the three types of motion may be run. See Diagram 6-8.

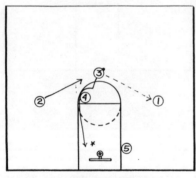
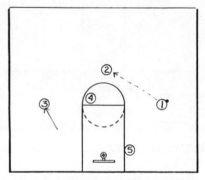

Diagram 6–7   **Diagram 6–8**

Dribble Entry Motion

The dribble entry is used when the defenders on the wing men are denying the entry pass. Diagram 6-9 is a continuation of the previous play sequence. Player (2) received a pass from (1). He has trouble passing to (3) or (1) at the wings, so he dribbles at (3).

This dribble key clears (3) to the far wing position. Player (2) then attempts to reverse the ball to him by way of (1), who replaced (2) at the point. See Diagram 6-10.

The pass from (1) to (3) would then key the lob play. See Diagram 6-11.

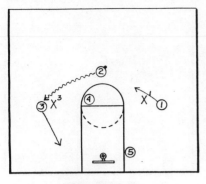

Diagram 6-9

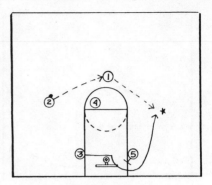

Diagram 6-10

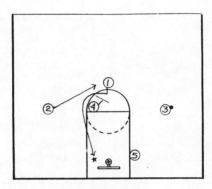

Diagram 6-11

The Set Play Phase

The three wheel patterns are run interchangeably until a set play is called by one of the perimeter players (1), (2), or (3). They do this by forming an overload. An example is shown in Diagram 6-12. Player (1) passes to (3), runs the lob cut, and then cuts to the ballside corner. This overload by the perimeter players tells both post men to move to the ballside. See Diagram 6-13.

Diagram 6-14 shows an overload being created after a slash cut and Diagram 6-15 shows an overload being created from a dribble entry key. Note that post man (5) moved to the ballside.

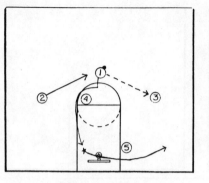

Diagram 6–12

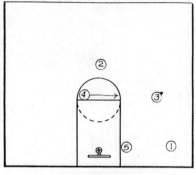

Diagram 6–13

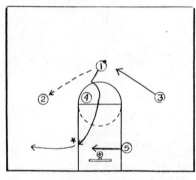

Diagram 6–14

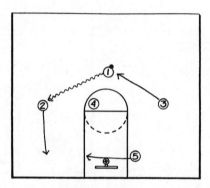

Diagram 6–15

From these overload formations, the following two set plays may be run:

Set Play #1—The Corner Play

In Diagram 6-16, (3) passes to (1) in the corner and cuts through.

Player (5) then steps out and works a screen-and-roll play with (1); (1) dribbles off (5) and may: (A) shoot or pass to (5) on the roll (see Diagram 6-17), or (B) pass to (3), who has looped around a double downscreen set by (4) and (2) (see Diagram 6-18).

Once (3) has received the pass from (1) and is not open, (2) cuts to the open wing, (4) moves high, and the Wheel Motions may be resumed. See Diagram 6-19.

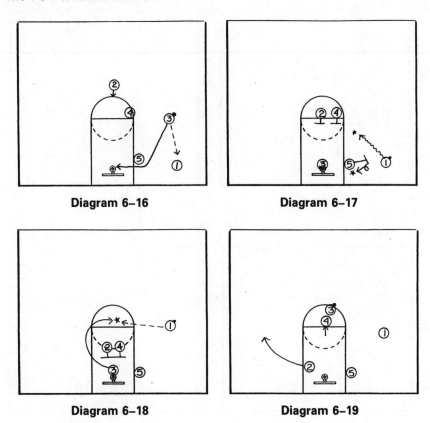

Diagram 6–16   **Diagram 6–17**

Diagram 6–18   **Diagram 6–19**

Set Play #2—The Force-a-Switch Play

At the time the overload was created, (3) had the ball at the wing and the offense had assumed the overload formation shown in Diagram 6-20.

To key the "Force-a-Switch Play," (3) passes to (4) at the high post. Player (5) steps out and screens for (1), who cuts to the basket looking for a pass. See Diagram 6-21.

In setting this screen, (5)'s goal is to force a switch. This leaves him being guarded by small defender X1, who is in bad position to stop a pass inside by (4). See Diagram 6-22.

If neither (1) nor (5) was open, it was probably because X5 and X1 fought hard to assume ballside and high defensive positions. When this happens, (4) can pass to either wing and change the passing angle to facilitate a pass inside. Diagram 6-23 shows (4) passing to (3). Player (3) then passes inside to (5) for a power lay-up shot.

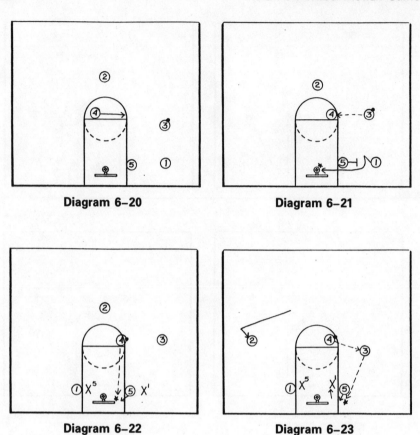

Diagram 6–20   Diagram 6–21

Diagram 6–22   Diagram 6–23

This same passing angle change may occur on the other side. Diagram 6-24 shows (4) passing to (2), and (2) passing inside to (1) for a power lay-up shot.

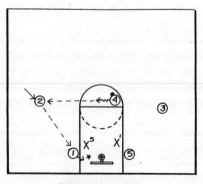

Diagram 6–24

PRESSURE RELIEVERS

At the time when the set plays may be run, the defense tends to overplay and three lob plays may be run to ease the pressure.

Lob to Low Post

Many teams have the defensive rule that requires their defenders to front all low post men. However, in this formation there is no offside help. This permits (3) to lob to (5) in Diagram 6-25.

Lob to High Post

Once the "Force-a-Switch Play" has been run, X4 will tend to overplay (4). When this happens (as shown in Diagram 6-26), (3) fakes to (4), (4) backdoors, and then (3) lobs to him.

If (4) is a good jump shooter and (5) a strong post man, X4 has quite a dilemma. If he helps on (5), (3) will pass to (4) for a jump shot. If X4 plays tight on (4), (3) may lob to (5) or (4).

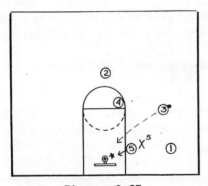   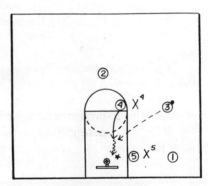

Diagram 6–25   **Diagram 6–26**

Lob to Point Man

In Diagram 6-27, the overload was formed and the offside wing man (2) has drifted to the point. Player (3) fakes a pass to (2) and this tells (2) to make a change of direction and cut off (4) to the offside lay-up slot. If (2) is open, (3) throws a lob pass to him.

These three lob passes tend to take away some of the defensive pressure.

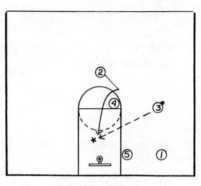

Diagram 6–27

AUXILIARY PLAYS

Offside Lob Play

This play starts in the same manner as the slash cut. To avoid confusion, it is called by a hand signal. In Diagram 6-28, point man (1) passes to wing man (2). The offside wing man (3) then cuts off the low post man to the ballside lay-up area.

If (3) is not open, he clears to the ballside corner, (4) drops low, and (5) moves up to screen for (1). See Diagram 6-29.

Player (2) then fakes to (1). This tells (1) to make a change of direction and cut to the offside lay-up area for a possible lob pass from (2). See Diagram 6-30.

If (1) is not open, he moves to the offside wing area. The team may now run one of the set plays.

Change-of-Assignments Lob Play

This play is run when the two post men (4) and (5) are being dominated by their defenders, and the team's guards (1) and (2) are strong inside. The play begins as the lob motion play, but when (1) passes to (3), the offside wing man (2) cuts off (4) to the high post area. See Diagram 6-31. Because its beginning is similar to the lob motion, it must be called with an oral or hand signal. Player (2)'s cut completely clears the offside help defenders and makes (1)'s subsequent cut a more viable one. See Diagram 6-32.

If (1) is not open, (4) steps out front to receive a pass from (3). At the same time, (5) swings across the lane to the wing position on that side. See Diagram 6-33.

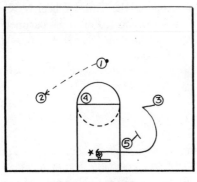

Diagram 6–28

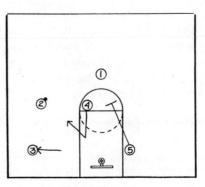

Diagram 6–29

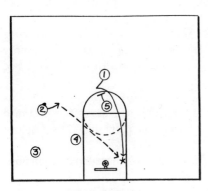

Diagram 6–30

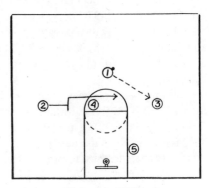

Diagram 6–31

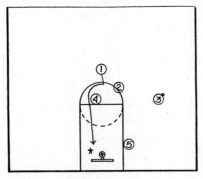

Diagram 6–32

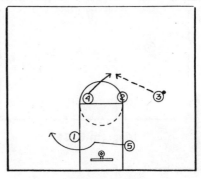

Diagram 6–33

The team is now in position to resume one of the Three Wheel Motion Plays. The difference is that the two post men (4) and (5) are now perimeter players, and (1) and (2) have assumed the post assignments. See Diagram 6-34.

Diagram 6-35 shows (4) keying the slash motion.

This change-of-positions play will hopefully take the two big dominating defenders covering (4) and (5) out of the lane area.

Point Lob Motion

This motion may be used as an alternative to the lob cut motion. It begins as point man (1) passes to the wing man on the low post side, and then cuts off high post man (4) for a possible lob pass. Wing man (2) uses (1)'s cut and high post man (4) to get open as he moves to the ballside high post area. See Diagram 6-36.

Player (3) looks first for (1) and then passes to (2) at the head of the key. At this point, a wheel effect takes place with (3) cutting over (5) as (1) clears under (5). See Diagram 6-37.

Player (2) may then pass to (3) going over the top, or (1) coming to the wing after looping under (5). If neither (3) nor (1) is open, (2) may wait for (4) to move down and screen for (3), to allow him to pop to the wing area on that side. See Diagram 6-38.

From there, (2) may pass to either wing man, (3) or (1). In making this pass, (2) always dribbles toward the desired side. This tells the offside post man ((5) in Diagram 6-39) to move high. It also permits the point man (2) to improve his passing angle to the desired wing.

If (2) had dribbled toward (1)'s side, (4) would have moved to the high post. See Diagram 6-40.

From there, the motion would resume. See Diagram 6-41.

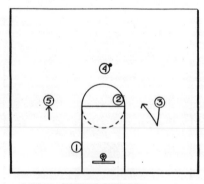

Diagram 6-34

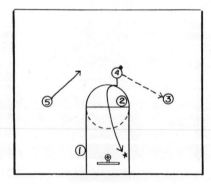

Diagram 6-35

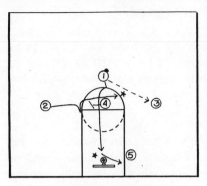

Diagram 6–36

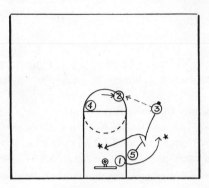

Diagram 6–37

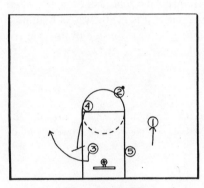

Diagram 6–38

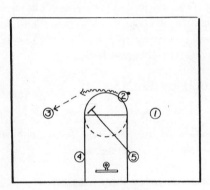

Diagram 6–39

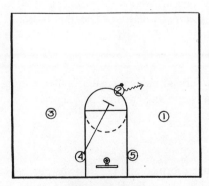

Diagram 6–40

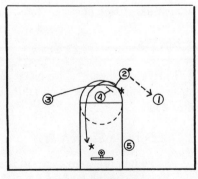

Diagram 6–41

VERSUS ZONE DEFENSES

The Wheel Motion, with a few minor adjustments, may be run against zone defenses. The three basic motion plays may be run with no changes. During the motion of these plays, the following scoring options will occur against zones.

Slash Cut Motion

In Diagram 6-42, (1) passes to wing man (2) and cuts through. He is then replaced at the point by the offside wing man (3). Player (1) then loops around low post man (5). Versus zones, (5) may attempt to trap the zone inside by screening the nearest zone player. The ball is then reversed from (1) to (3) to (2) for a possible jump shot.

At all times, the three perimeter players are aware that a pass to the high post (4) may lead to the low post's being open inside the zone. For example, when running this play, it is also possible to reverse the ball to (1) by way of high post man (4). He receives a pass from (2) and may pass to (5) inside or to (1) at the wing. See Diagram 6-43.

Lob Play Motion

The Lob Play has no definite scoring options against zones. However, the motion of this play will force zones to adjust. This is particularly true of matching zone defenses.

Dribble Entry Play Motion

The Dribble Entry Play is especially effective when used on the wing at the high post man's side of the court ((2) in Diagram 6-44). Player (1) dribbles at (2) and may clear him to the ballside corner to form an overload (see Diagram 6-45), or around the offside post man for a quick reversal play (see Diagram 6-46).

The Set Plays

During the three motion plays, an overload may be created by the cutter going to the ballside corner. Once this occurs, the set plays may be adapted to run against zones.

The Force-a-Switch Play

In Diagram 6-47, an overload has been formed and (2) calls the Force-a-Switch Play by passing to (4) at the high post. This tells (1) to cut off (5) and (3) to move to the offside wing. Player (1)'s cut has little use against zones, but (5) is very often open inside the zone. If (5) is not open, (4) looks for (3) at the far wing position.

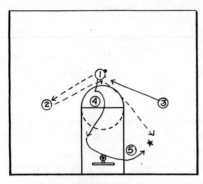

Diagram 6-42

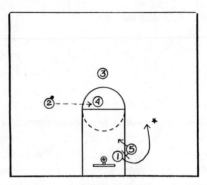

Diagram 6-43

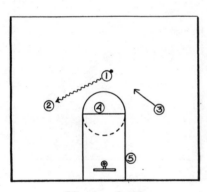

Diagram 6-44

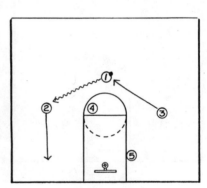

Diagram 6-45

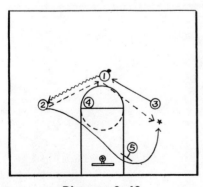

Diagram 6-46

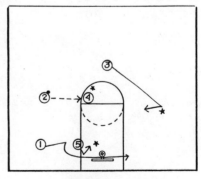

Diagram 6-47

The Corner Play

The overload has been formed and this time (2) chooses to pass to (1) in the corner. Player (2) then cuts through. Against zones, (4), the high post man, moves down to screen for (2), and (3) stays at the point. See Diagram 6-48.

Player (1) then dribbles off (5) and may shoot, pass to (5) inside, or reverse the ball to (2) by way of (3). See Diagram 6-49.

Thus, with a few adjustments, the three wheel motions and two set plays may be run against zone defenses. They test the zone by forcing it to cover overloads, overshifts, high to low post passes, and screens.

The Wheel Motion Offense moves the defense in three probing patterns that may provide easy shots. By the time an overload is formed, the defense may have relaxed and the Set Plays will be very difficult for them to cover. This offense, with a few simple adjustments, also works well versus zone defenses.

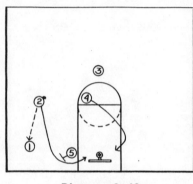

Diagram 6-48

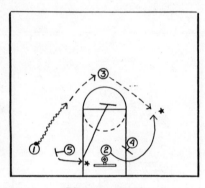

Diagram 6-49

CHAPTER 7

The Lob Motion

This motion is an abbreviated continuity in that players (4) and (5) remain in the pivot areas and (1), (2), and (3) move around the perimeter. It is based around three of the most difficult maneuvers to defense. They are the offside screen and cut, the UCLA slash, and a backscreen that results in a lob pass.

PERSONNEL ALIGNMENT

Players (4) and (5) should be tall and able to leap to receive lob passes. Players (1), (2), and (3) should be mobile, but need not be very tall. The onside post man ((4) in Diagram 7-1) always sets up high and the offside post man (5) sets up low.

THE BASIC MOTION

The Basic Motion—Key #1

In Diagram 7-2, (1) passes to (2) and does not cut. This tells the offside wing man (3) to cut off (5) to the ballside post area. Following (3)'s cut, (5) steps up and screens (4)'s man. Player (4) cuts to the offside lay-up slot for a possible lob pass from (2).

Player (2) looks first for (3), then for (4) on the lob. If neither is open, (2) passes to (1) at the point and he and (5) screen down for (3), who pops to the wing for a possible pass from (1). Note that (1) had made a change of direction to keep his defender busy. See Diagram 7-3.

After screening for (3), (2) continues across the lane and loops around (4) to the wing and receives a pass from (1). This pass makes (4) the onside post man so he sets up high. It also makes (5) the offside post man so he remains low. See Diagram 7-4.

The pattern is then repeated with (3) cutting off (5) and (5) screening for (4) to facilitate the lob pass. See Diagrams 7-5 and 7-6.

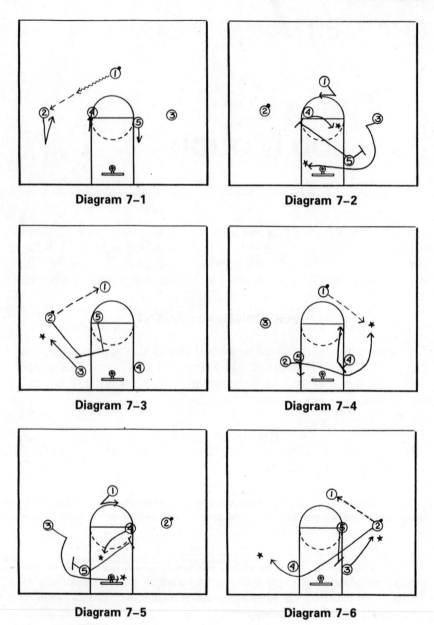

Diagram 7–1

Diagram 7–2

Diagram 7–3

Diagram 7–4

Diagram 7–5

Diagram 7–6

The Basic Motion—Key #2

This time, (1) passes to wing man (2) and slash cuts off high post man (4) and to the ballside low post area. This tells (3) not to cut off (5), but to replace (1) at the point. See Diagram 7-7.

From there, the options are the same with (3) and (1) exchanging assignments. See Diagrams 7-8 and 7-9.

Alternate Motion Keying Method

Another method of keying the motion is to have (1) pass to a wing (as to (2) in Diagram 7-10) and screen away for the offside wing man (3). From there, two things may occur: (A) player (3) may ignore (1)'s screen and cut off (5). This tells (1) to cut back to the point. Or (B), player (3) may utilize (1)'s screen and cut to the point. This tells (1) to roll to the ballside post area. See Diagram 7-11.

Either of these options leaves the players in position to continue the basic pattern.

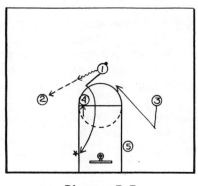

Diagram 7–7

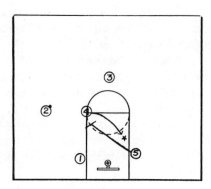

Diagram 7–8

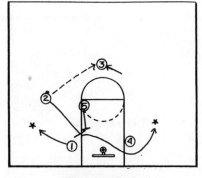

Diagram 7–9

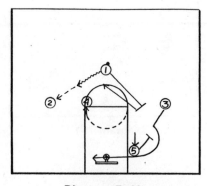

Diagram 7–10

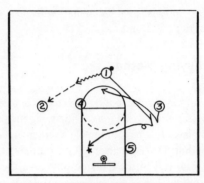

Diagram 7–11

Post Reversal Option

Once the motion has been initiated and a player has cut to the ballside low post area, the wing with the ball ((2) in Diagram 7-12) may also pass to the high post (5). See Diagrams 7-12 and 7-13.

When this pass occurs, (2) still screens down for the player in the ballside low post area. Player (1) pops to the ballside wing and (5) may pass to (1) popping out, (4) posting up, or, as shown in Diagram 7-14, to (2) looping to the offside wing.

Player (5)'s pass to (2) tells him to drop low and (4) to set up high. From there, the basic motion is repeated. See Diagrams 7-15 and 7-16.

These plays make up the back motion.

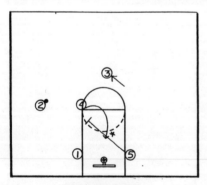

Diagram 7–12

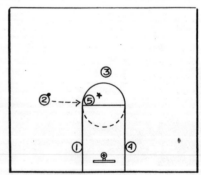

Diagram 7–13

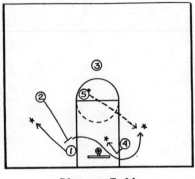

Diagram 7–14

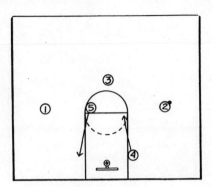

Diagram 7–15

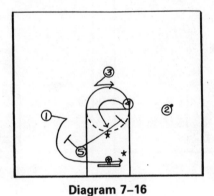

Diagram 7–16

PRESSURE RELIEVERS

Strongside Dribble Entry

When the initial passes to the wing are being denied, (1) may dribble at a wing man (as at (2) in Diagram 7-17). This tells (2) to loop around the high post man and to the point. Seeing (1)'s dribble entry, (3) cuts off (5) and to the ballside low post area.

From there, the basic motion options may prevail. See Diagrams 7-18 through 7-20.

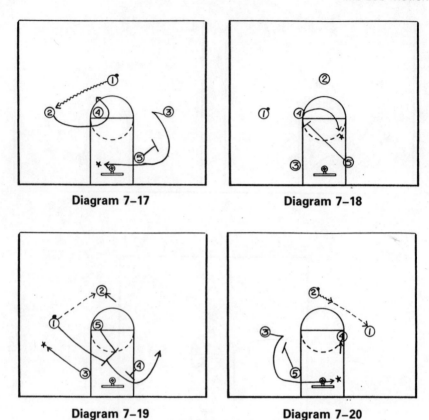

Diagram 7–17   Diagram 7–18

Diagram 7–19   Diagram 7–20

Reversal Point-to-Wing Pass Denied

When the point-to-wing pass that reverses the ball and resets the offense is being denied, the following dribble entry may be employed. In Diagram 7-21, (1) has received a pass from (2). This time, instead of waiting for (2) to move to the offside wing, (1) makes an immediate dribble entry.

This dribble entry tells (2) to replace (1) at the point. See Diagram 7-22. From there, the basic options of the motion may be resumed.

Pass-to-the-Post Backdoor Play

Another device that may be utilized when the defense is denying passes to the wings is a pass to the post. In Diagram 7-23, (1) can pass to neither wing so he bounce passes to the high post man (4).

This tells the onside wing man (2) to backdoor his defender and (1) to make a change of direction and become the second man through. See Diagram 7-24.

It also tells the offside wing man to make a change of direction and cut to the point off a screen by (5). He becomes the third option. See Diagram 7-25.

The final option comes as (2) continues his cut across the lane and loops around (5) for a pass from (4). See Diagram 7-26.

From there, the basic motion is started as (4) drops low, (5) cuts high, and (1) cuts off (4). See Diagrams 7-27 and 7-28.

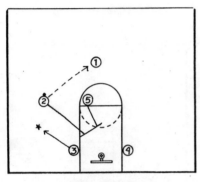

Diagram 7–21

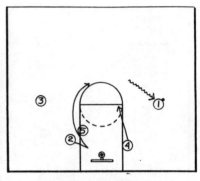

Diagram 7–22

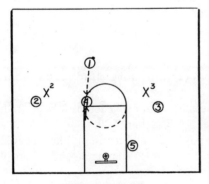

Diagram 7–23

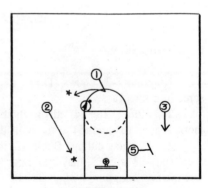

Diagram 7–24

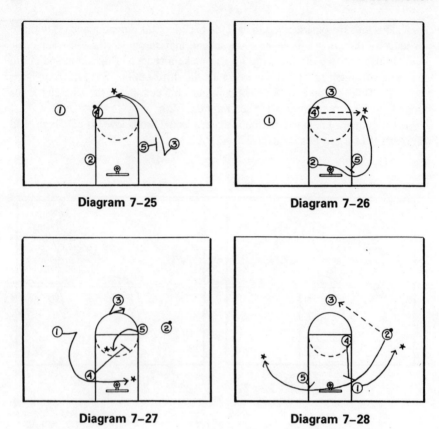

Diagram 7-25   **Diagram 7-26**

Diagram 7-27   **Diagram 7-28**

AUXILIARY PLAYS

Post Loop Play

Diagram 7-29 shows (1) passing to (2), (3) cutting off (5), and (5) blind screening for (4).

This time, after (4) cuts to the basket for a possible lob pass from (2), he loops around (3) and (5) to the ballside. See Diagram 7-30.

This looping cut by (4) tells (2) to pass to (1) and cut over (5) for a possible return pass. Player (1) may then pass to (2) or to (4) coming around the double screen. See Diagram 7-31.

Five-Man X Motion

If you desire to run a five-man motion in conjunction with the lob motion, the Five-Man X Motion will suffice. This offensive plan moves all five defenders

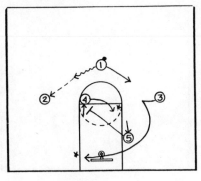

Diagram 7-29

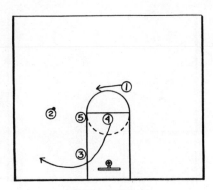

Diagram 7-30

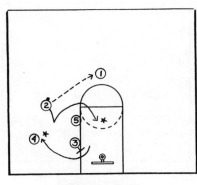

Diagram 7-31

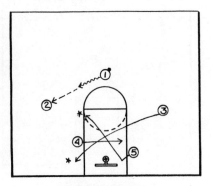

Diagram 7-32

in a five-man continuity and should be used when the defense is dominating the lane area.

Diagram 7-32 shows (1) passing to wing man (2). This tells the onside post man (4) to cut to the far side of the lane, and above the post man (5) on that side. Wing man (3) and post man (5) then use (4)'s cut with (3) cutting first over (4) and to a low post position. Post man (5) uses (3)'s cut as a natural screen and cuts to the ballside high post area.

Following the X cut by players (3) and (5), (1) moves down to screen for (4), who pops to the point to receive a pass from (2). See Diagram 7-33.

After passing to (4), (2) joins (5) in a double screen down for (3), who pops to the wing area. Player (2) then crosses the lane and uses (1) as a natural screen as he moves to the wing area on that side. See Diagram 7-34.

Player (1) may then pass to either wing (as to (2) in Diagram 7-35), and the motion will be repeated. See Diagrams 7-36 and 7-37.

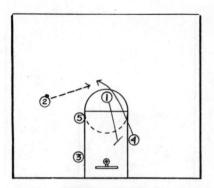

Diagram 7–33

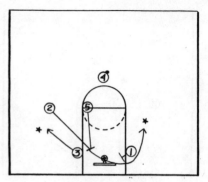

Diagram 7–34

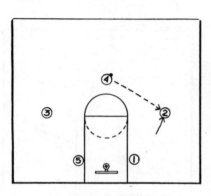

Diagram 7–35

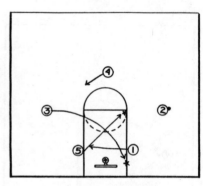

Diagram 7–36

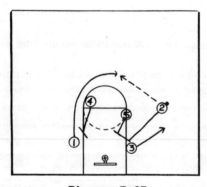

Diagram 7–37

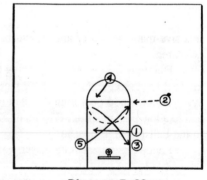

Diagram 7–38

Force-the-Switch Play

As the X continuity progresses, a pass from the wing to the high post man ((5) in Diagram 7-38) calls the Force-the-Switch Play.

This pass tells (3) to step out and screen (2)'s defender (X2) and attempt to force a switch. Player (5) looks first for (2) and a possible lob pass. See Diagram 7-39.

If the lob pass is not open, (3) rolls inside and posts up (hopefully with X2 guarding him and in poor defensive position). See Diagram 7-40.

If (3) is not open, (2) loops around (4) to the offside wing and (5) passes to him. This tells (4) to screen away for (5) and (3), who execute the X pattern. See Diagrams 7-41 through 7-43.

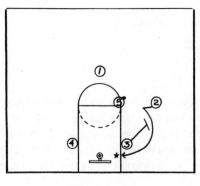

Diagram 7–39

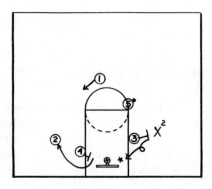

Diagram 7–40

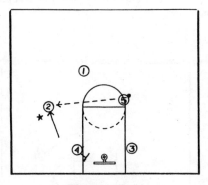

Diagram 7–41

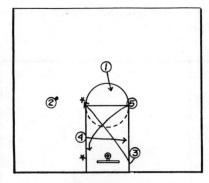

Diagram 7–42

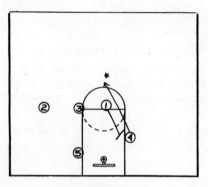

Diagram 7–43

VERSUS ZONE DEFENSES

The Basic Motion

It is best to start this motion against zones by making a pass to the wing on the low post side. This shifts the zone in that direction. See Diagram 7-44.

Then, as the ball is quickly reversed to the other wing man (2) by way of point man (1), (5) steps up and screens the overshift. See Diagram 7-45. Player (3) uses this screen and cuts to the basket for a possible lob pass. See Diagram 7-46.

If (3) is not open, he continues across the lane. At the same time, (5) cuts to the ballside as (4) cuts over him to the offside low post area. This lob motion has little utility versus zones, but if (2) can pass to (5), either (3) or (4) may be open inside the zone. See Diagrams 7-47 and 7-48.

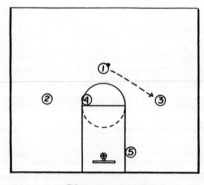

Diagram 7–44

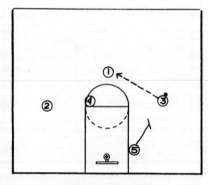

Diagram 7–45

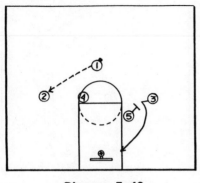

Diagram 7-46

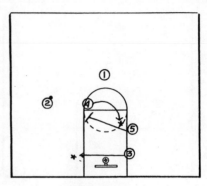

Diagram 7-47

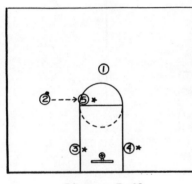

Diagram 7-48

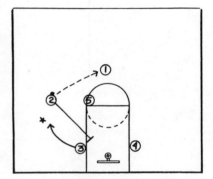

Diagram 7-49

It should be mentioned that the time needed for the above play sequence results in (2) holding the ball for an inordinate amount of time. If (2) feels pressure, he may pass to (1) and receive a return pass.

If (2) cannot pass to (5), he passes to (1) at the point and attempts to trap the zone inside by screening down for (3), who has moved halfway to the ballside corner. See Diagram 7-49.

Player (1) may then: (A) pass to (3) at the wing, (B) pass to (5), who would shoot or look inside for (2) or (4) (Diagram 7-50), or (C) fake to (3) and take a dribble toward the far wing. This move tells (2) to clear across the lane and around (4)'s screen. Player (4) attempts to trap the zone inside by screening the nearest zone player. See Diagram 7-51.

As (1) dribbled, (5) moved low, and (4) cut high. From there, (1)'s pass to (2) restarts the motion. See Diagram 7-52.

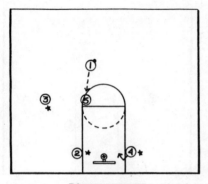

Diagram 7-50

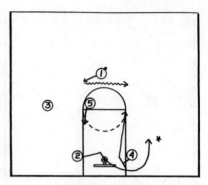

Diagram 7-51

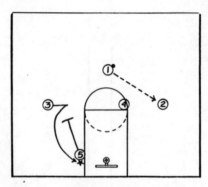

Diagram 7-52

This lob-oriented motion involves many basic functional play components. It is, in the main, an abbreviated continuity with big players (4) and (5) staying close to the basket and the more mobile players (1), (2), and (3) in continuous motion on the perimeter. If the two big men are being dominated inside by their defenders, the Five-Man X Motion may be added. The offense with a few simple adjustments may be run against zone defenses.

CHAPTER 8

The De Paul Cut Motion Offense

A very popular motion that moves the defense in a functional manner is the De Paul Cut Motion. It works well versus man-to-man and zone defenses.

PERSONNEL ALIGNMENT

This motion is designed for two guard types (1) and (2), two forwards (3) and (4) who have adequate size and shooting ability, and a big post man (5), who can dominate the low post area in terms of one-on-one scoring and rebounding. The guards should be positioned as wide as the lane. The ballside forward (3) in Diagram 8-1 is as high as the free throw line extended and the offside forward (4) is situated in the offside low post area.

THE BASIC MOTION

Player (3) must be open in his assigned area when (1) picks up his dribble. He can get open by: (A) stacking under (5) as the ball comes upcourt and popping to the wing at the appropriate time (Diagram 8-2), (B) facing his defender X3 and then cutting away to the wing (Diagram 8-3), (C) moving up the lane and then cutting directly out to the wing (Diagram 8-4), or (D), in cases of extreme defensive pressure, crossing with (4) to move the defense (see Diagram 8-5).

Once the pass to (3) is made, (1) cuts to the offside lay-up slot off a screen by (4), who moved to the high post area. See Diagram 8-6.

Player (3) may then: (A) Lob to (1). (B) Pass to (5) and split the post with (4). When this is done, (4) steps out and sets a definite screen for (3). Player (3) uses the screen to cut into the lane and (4) rolls to the ball. See Diagram 8-7. (C) Pass to (2) and cut low off (5) after (2) passes to (1). See Diagram 8-8. Or, (D) pass to (2) and cut high off (4). See Diagram 8-9.

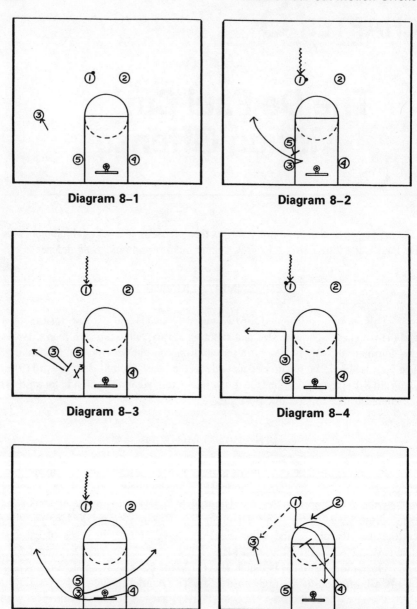

Diagram 8–1   Diagram 8–2

Diagram 8–3   Diagram 8–4

Diagram 8–5   Diagram 8–6

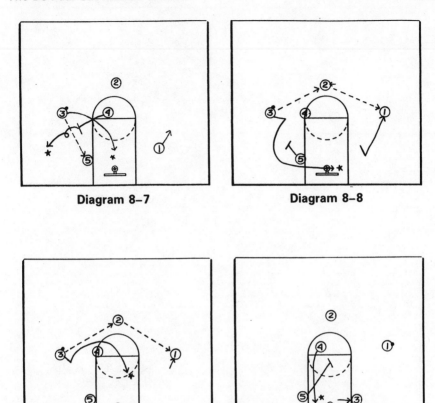

Diagram 8-7   **Diagram 8-8**

Diagram 8-9   **Diagram 8-10**

Player (1) then has the options of: (A) passing to (3) cutting to the ballside low post area, (B) lobbing to (4) who moved low off (5)'s screen (Diagram 8-10), (C) passing to (5) moving to the ballside after his screen for (4) (Diagram 8-11), or (D) resetting the offense. Player (1) can do this by dribbling out front and then passing to (3), popping out of (5)'s downscreen. See Diagrams 8-12 and 8-13.

When resetting the offense, (1) may also pass to (2) and then loop around (4) to the offside guard position. Player (2) then dribbles to the ballside and passes to (3) to initiate the motion. See Diagrams 8-14 and 8-15.

From there, the basic options of the motion would again be open.

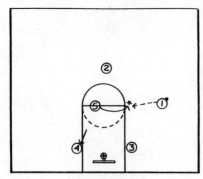

Diagram 8–11

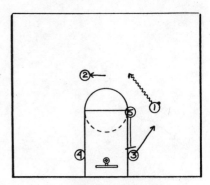

Diagram 8–12

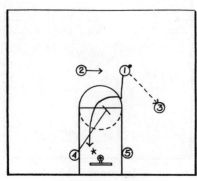

Diagram 8–13

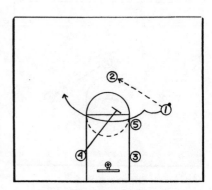

Diagram 8–14

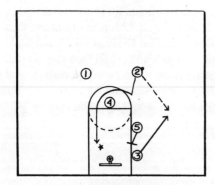

Diagram 8–15

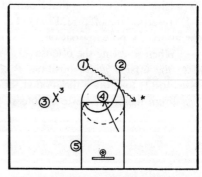

Diagram 8–16

PRESSURE RELIEVERS

Initial Entry Pass Denied

Diagram 8-16 shows (1) unable to pass to (3), the forward on his side. Seeing this, (2) clears down and around (4), who has cut to the high post. This allows (1) to make a dribble entry on the weakside.

Player (3) then makes his cut off (5) to what is now the ballside. See Diagram 8-17. Player (5) screens for (4) for the lob option. See Diagram 8-18.

The end result is that the motion has been run without the guard lob option. If no shot develops, (1) passes out to (2), and the offense is reset.

The same play may be run when the weakside guard brings the ball upcourt. He can make a dribble entry and the basic motion is run excluding the first option. See Diagrams 8-19 through 8-21.

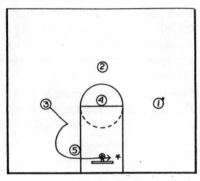

Diagram 8–17

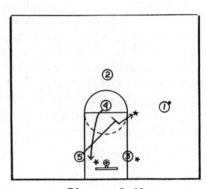

Diagram 8–18

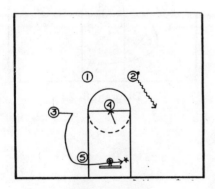

Diagram 8–19

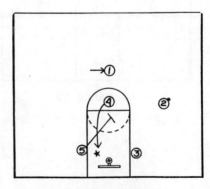

Diagram 8–20

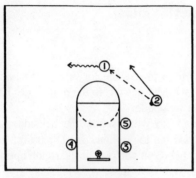

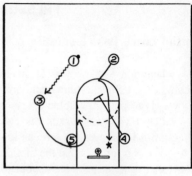

Diagram 8–21   Diagram 8–22

Dribble Entry (Initial Entry Pass Denied)

Diagram 8-22 shows (1) unable to pass to (3), who is being overplayed. Player (1) dribbles at (3) and clears him down and around the low post man (5) and to the point. Player (2) moves toward the ball, backdoor cuts off (4)'s screen, and moves to the offside lay-up area for a possible lob from (1).

If (2) is not open, (1) passes to (3), who reverses the ball to (2), who has by then moved to the offside wing area. See Diagram 8-23.

Player (1) cuts off (5) to the ballside lay-up area. See Diagram 8-24. Then (5) screens for (4) for the lob option. See Diagram 8-25. If nothing develops, (2) passes to (3) and the motion is reset.

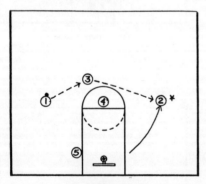

Diagram 8–23   Diagram 8–24

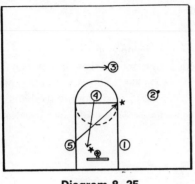
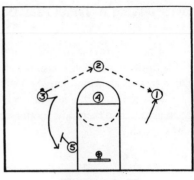

Diagram 8–25   **Diagram 8–26**

Reversal Denied

When it is difficult to reverse the ball, it must be remembered that three methods may be used to get the ball from wing to wing. Diagram 8-26 shows the standard method. Diagram 8-27 shows the reversal by way of the offside forward (4), and Diagram 8-28 shows a direct "skip" pass that is made possible because (1)'s defender X1 is helping in the lane.

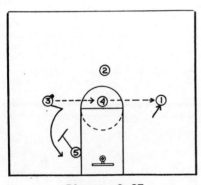
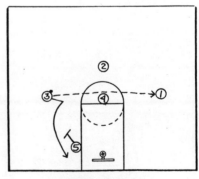

Diagram 8–27   **Diagram 8–28**

Point-to-Wing Reversal Pass Denied

When the reversal is denied at the time in the motion that the point-to-wing pass is thrown, a dribble chase may be used. Diagram 8-29 shows point man (2) unable to pass to wing man (1). He dribbles at (1) and clears him to the point.

This tells the offside wing man (3) to cut off (5) and move to the ballside lay-up area. From there, the motion options are the same as usual. See Diagrams 8-30 through 8-32.

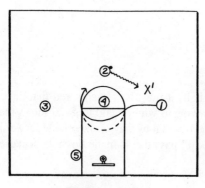

Diagram 8–29

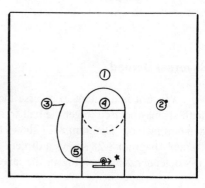

Diagram 8–30

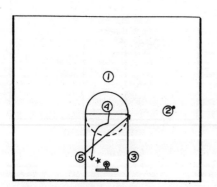

Diagram 8–31

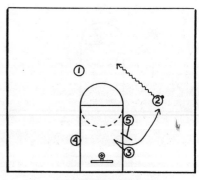

Diagram 8–32

AUXILIARY PLAYS

Multi-Option Split Play

In Diagram 8-33, (3) is being denied so (1) bounce passes to low post man (5), who moves toward the pass. This tells (3) to backdoor X3, and (1) and (2) to split off (4).

Player (5) may then shoot, pass to (3) on the backdoor cut, look for (1) cutting off (4), or pass to (2) for a jump shot.

Dribble Entry Lob Play

This play is keyed when guard (1) dribbles at forward (3) and clears him to the lane, over forward (4), and to the offside lay-up area for a possible lob pass. See Diagram 8-34.

Player (1) may lob to (3) or reverse the ball to him and key the subsequent options. See Diagrams 8-35 and 8-36.

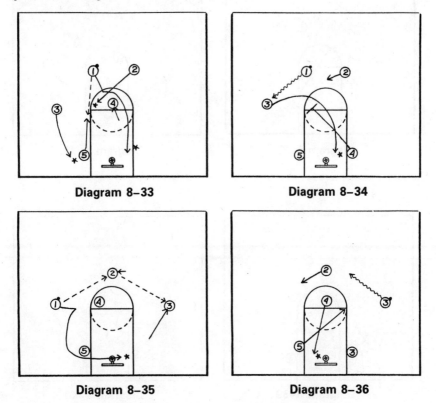

Diagram 8–33   Diagram 8–34

Diagram 8–35   Diagram 8–36

Chicago Option

When initiating the play, (1) may use an old Chicago Bull (NBA) option. After his pass to (3), he moves down and screens for (4), who delays and then cuts to the high post and receives a pass from (3). See Diagram 8-37. He, (4), may shoot or pass to (5), who forced a switch by setting a definite screen on (3)'s defender and forced X5 to pick up the open cutter. See Diagram 8-38.

This left (5) inside small defender X5 for a possible lob pass. See Diagram 8-39.

Player (4) may also fake a pass to (3) and force X5 to play ballside and high. A subsequent pass to (1) creates an angle for him to pass to (3) inside X5 for a power lay-up. See Diagram 8-40.

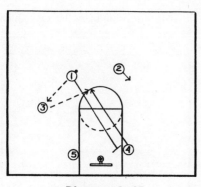

Diagram 8-37

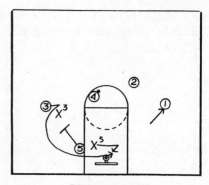

Diagram 8-38

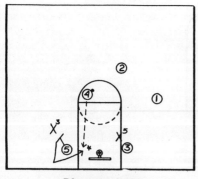

Diagram 8-39

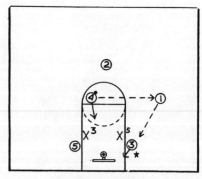

Diagram 8-40

VERSUS ZONE DEFENSES

Chicago Option

When using the De Paul Cut Motion versus zones, the Chicago option works best. Diagram 8-41 shows (1) pass to (3), and cut through. This tells the offside forward to cut to the high post. Player (1)'s cut changed the offensive front from even to odd. This causes matching zones to make adjustments. Player (4)'s cut to the high post may result in a triangle play with (4) at the apex and the base formed by (5) and (1) inside the zone. See Diagram 8-42.

If (4) is not open, he continues his cut to the ballside of the lane. Player (3) reverses the ball from (2) to (1), who has moved to the wing area. See Diagram 8-43.

Player (3) then cuts high off (4) to the free throw line area. If (1) can pass to (3), he may shoot, pass inside to (5), or pass to (4), who has moved to the offside wing. See Diagram 8-44.

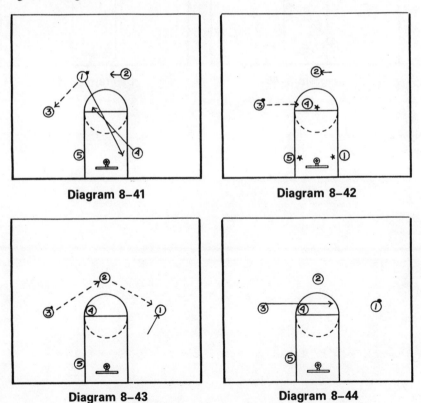

Diagram 8-41

Diagram 8-42

Diagram 8-43

Diagram 8-44

If (1) cannot pass to (3), (3) continues his cut to the ballside low post area. Player (5) then cuts to the ballside high post area. See Diagram 8-45.

Again, if the pass is made to (5), he can shoot, pass to (3) inside, or reverse the ball to (4) on the offside wing. See Diagram 8-46.

If (1) cannot pass to (5), he dribbles out front and returns the offense to a two-man front. From there, the Chicago option zone sequence may be repeated.

The De Paul Cut Motion is a method of utilizing a big post man, (5), within the context of movement. It is easy to teach and adaptable to zone defenses by way of the Chicago option.

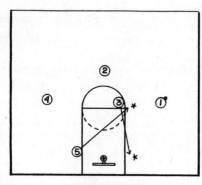

Diagram 8-45

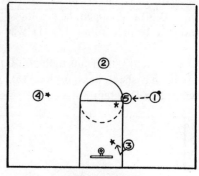

Diagram 8-46

CHAPTER 9

A Disciplined Flex Control Motion

In my book *Modern Basketball Team Techniques,* I stressed that a team choosing to employ a ball control offense will have many advantages over the running team. Some of them are:

- Forcing the opposition to spend an inordinate amount of time playing defense will often cause them to tire in the latter stages of the game.
- Teams tend to accumulate more fouls when they are on defense.
- At the end of most close games both teams will resort to a more controlled style of play and attempt to "set it up." The control team has more experience at this style of play and should gain an advantage.
- A wide open running team's offense is usually initiated by a big rebounder's outlet pass. He will make more errors than the highly skilled guard who keys the plays of a control team.
- The tall people who dominate the game of basketball are not adept at being defenders in a game of "keep away."
- And, finally, the nature of the game of basketball, and the way the rules are interpreted tend to favor the team with the ball.

The following disciplined control game is predicated on those ideas and designed around the UCLA Slash Play and the Flex Motion.

PERSONNEL ALIGNMENT

Guards (1) and (2) bring the ball upcourt and then (2) cuts to the strongside forward area. Forwards (3) and (4) assume the guard and forward positions on the other side. Post man (5) sets up in the high post on the ballside. See Diagram 9-1.

This alignment is based on the assumption that (1) and (2) are the team's best ballhandlers.

THE BASIC MOTIONS

UCLA Slash Delay Motion

In Diagram 9-2, (1) passes to (2), makes a slash cut off (5), and on to the ballside lay-up slot, for a possible pass from (2). It must be remembered that this is a ball control game and (2)'s rule on this pass is "if in doubt, don't."

If (1) does not receive a pass from (2), he clears to the ballside corner, and (5) rolls toward the basket. See Diagram 9-3.

If (5) is not open, (2) dribbles out front and this tells (1) to make a change of direction and cut to the ballside forward area, and the two offside players (3) and (4) to exchange positions. Note that after screening for (4), (3) rolled inside for a possible lob pass from (2). See Diagram 9-4.

The process is then repeated with (2) passing to (1), making the slash cut, and then (1) dribbling out front as (4) and (3) exchange. See Diagrams 9-5 and 9-6.

Note that (5) did not return to the high post until (2) passed to (1).

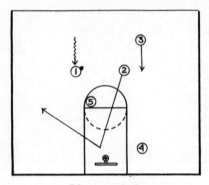

Diagram 9-1

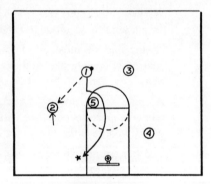

Diagram 9-2

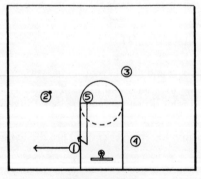

Diagram 9-3

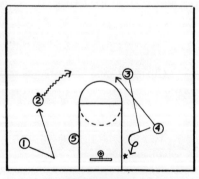

Diagram 9-4

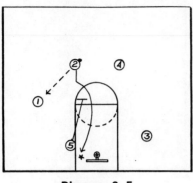

Diagram 9-5

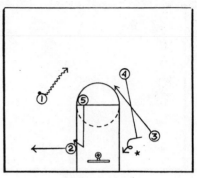

Diagram 9-6

Flex Motion

The second phase of this plan is the Flex Motion. The slash cut repetition tends to lull the defense into a relaxed state. It also sets them up for the Flex Motion. Diagram 9-7 shows that (1) has cut through and cleared to the ballside corner.

At that point, (2) dribbles out front and the Flex Motion is keyed by (2) passing to (4) who has exchanged positions with (3) and moved out front. See Diagram 9-8.

This pass tells (1) to cut off (5), who has stepped out to screen for him. See Diagram 9-9. If (1) is not open, (2) screens down for (5), who pops to the offside guard area. See Diagram 9-10.

From there, (4) has two basic options. He may pass to (5) and continue the Flex, or pass to (3) and run the slash cut delay game.

In Diagrams 9-11 and 9-12, (4) passes to (5) and keys the Flex Motion.

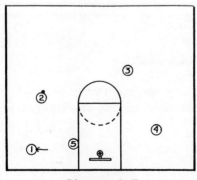

Diagram 9-7

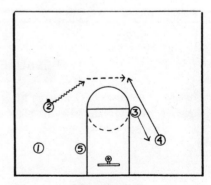

Diagram 9-8

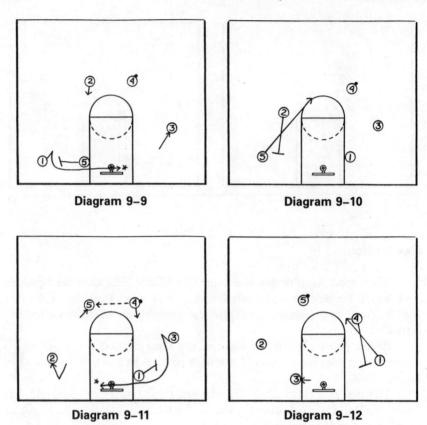

Diagram 9–9   Diagram 9–10

Diagram 9–11   Diagram 9–12

Slash Cut Delay Game

Diagram 9-13 shows (4) pass to (3) and cut off (1), who moved to the high post area. Player (3) then dribbles out front. This keys (5) and (2) to exchange on the offside. See Diagram 9-14. This delay phase teases and works the defense while setting up a flex option.

PRESSURE RELIEVERS

Most defenses have a tough time with this stalling, teasing offensive plan. However, two pressure-relieving plays are provided that may be necessary when facing a particularly strong defense.

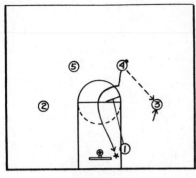
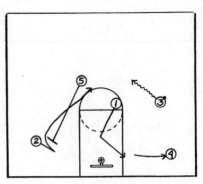

Diagram 9–13   **Diagram 9–14**

Pressure Reliever #1—Dribble Entry

When the defender on (2) denies the initial pass from (1), a dribble entry may be used. In Diagram 9-15, (1) dribbles at (2) and clears him down and around high post man (5). This tells (3) to cut over the post man (5) for a possible pass from (1), and a lay-up shot. Player (2) then cuts to the point. See Diagram 9-16.

If (3) is not open, he continues across the lane and around (4). Player (2) arrives at the ballside guard area and receives a pass from (1). See Diagram 9-17.

From there, either the slash cut delay game (see Diagram 9-18) or the flex motion may be keyed (see Diagram 9-19).

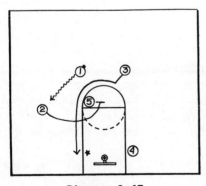
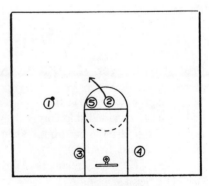

Diagram 9–15   **Diagram 9–16**

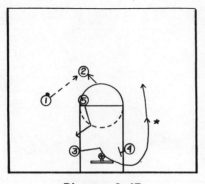

Diagram 9–17

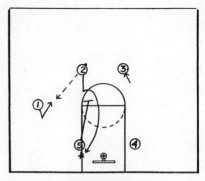

Diagram 9–18

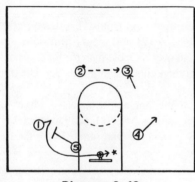

Diagram 9–19

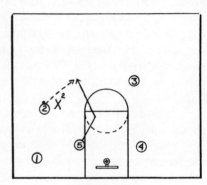

Diagram 9–20

Pressure Reliever #2—UCLA Downscreen

Diagram 9-20 shows that (1) has already made his slash cut (was not open) and cleared to the ballside corner. However, X2 is overplaying (2) and will not permit him to dribble out front. When this occurs, post man (5) steps out front and takes a pass from (2).

Player (2) then screens for (1), who pops to the wing, and receives a pass from (5). See Diagram 9-21.

As (1) dribbles out front, (5) returns to his low post position, (2) makes a change of direction, and then fills the forward position, and (3) and (4) exchange positions. See Diagram 9-22.

Player (1) may then call the Flex with a pass to (4) (see Diagram 9-23), or the Slash Delay Motion by passing to (2) (see Diagram 9-24).

Diagram 9-21

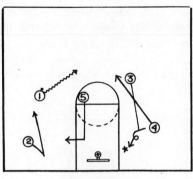

Diagram 9-22

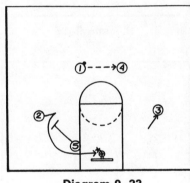

Diagram 9-23

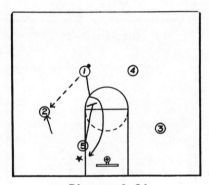

Diagram 9-24

AUXILIARY PLAYS

High Post Flex Play

Auxiliary plays may be added when a particular game demands them or as more offense is needed. Following are two plays that work well with the Flex Discipline Control Game.

When a player in the strongside guard position ((1) in Diagram 9-25) chooses to pass to high post man (5), both forwards (2) and (4) backdoor their defenders.

If neither (2) nor (4) is open, they cross underneath and receive down-screens from (1) and (3). See Diagram 9-26.

Player (5) may then pass to either (2) or (4). In Diagram 9-27, he chooses to pass to (2). This tells (3) to swing wide and (1) to blindscreen for (4).

Player (4) cuts to the basket off (1)'s screen, looking for a possible pass from (2). See Diagram 9-28. After (4)'s cut, (5) screens away for (1), who moves out front. See Diagram 9-29.

From there, (2) may continue the Flex Motion with a pass to (1) (see Diagram 9-30), or pass to (3) and key the Slash Delay Game (see Diagram 9-31).

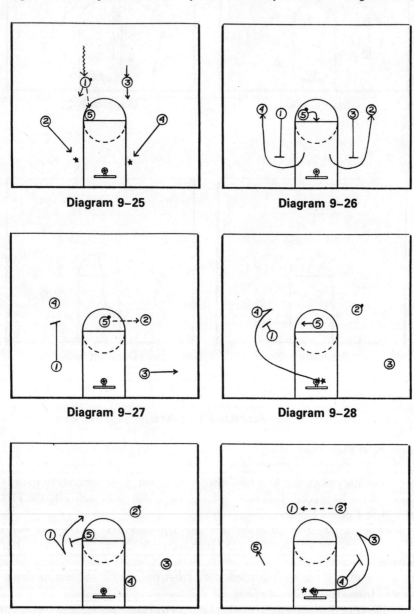

Diagram 9–25   **Diagram 9–26**

Diagram 9–27   **Diagram 9–28**

Diagram 9–29   **Diagram 9–30**

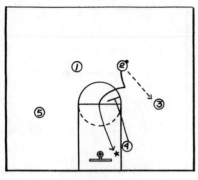

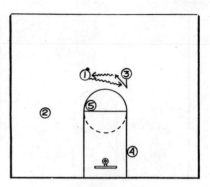

| Diagram 9-31 | Diagram 9-32 |

Backdoor Cross

When the defense is denying all the passes on the ballside, the Backdoor Cross may be run. In Diagram 9-32, (1) has no one to pass to, so he dribbles at (3). This tells (3) to fake a backdoor cut, come back, get the ball from (1), and dribble toward (2).

Player (2) reads this key and backdoors his defender (X2); (4) moves up and screens for (1). Player (3) may then pass to (2) on the backdoor cut, or lob to (1) on the offside. See Diagram 9-33.

If neither (2) nor (1) is open, they cross, with (2) setting a definite screen on (1)'s defender. Player (4) moves out front. See Diagram 9-34.

Player (3) may then pass to (1) and run the Slash Cut Delay Game (see Diagram 9-35), or pass to (4) and initiate the Flex Motion (see Diagram 9-36).

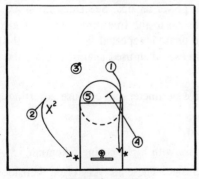
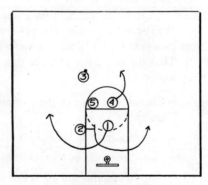

| Diagram 9-33 | Diagram 9-34 |

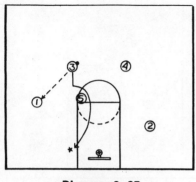

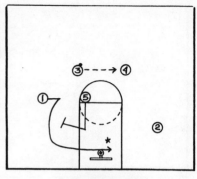

Diagram 9–35   **Diagram 9–36**

VERSUS ZONE DEFENSES

Zone Adjustments to Basic Motion

When using this offense against zone defenses, certain adjustments must be made. In Diagram 9-37, (1) passes to (2), slashes off high post man (5), and cuts to the corner. Post man (5) then drops down to form a passing triangle with (1) and (2). Player (3) does not move to the ballside, but instead stays wide and may be open for a crosscourt pass from (2) and an easy jump shot. See Diagram 9-38.

This triangle is maintained until (2) decides to switch the overload. He does this by dribbling at (3), and then passing to him. The two offside players (3) and (4) do not exchange because this maneuver has little utility versus zone defenses. See Diagram 9-39. The pass from (2) to (3) tells (1) to cut over the top of (5) and to the high post area.

If (3) can then get the ball to (1), a triangle play is formed with (1) at the apex and (4) and (5) forming the base. Player (1) may then turn and shoot or look for (4) or (5) inside the zone for possible power lay-ups. See Diagram 9-40.

If (3) cannot pass to (1), (4) breaks up to the free throw line extended, receives a pass from (3), and the slash cut phase is repeated. See Diagram 9-41.

Thus the two basic plays of this offense when used against zones allow a team to:

- Change the front of their offensive perimeter and confuse adjusting or matching zones.
- Utilize a passing triangle overload.
- Have the threat of a crosscourt pass with high scoring potential.
- Test the middle and corner of the zone. These are very often their most vulnerable areas.

– Rotate the perimeter of the zone by dribbling.

– Change the overload.

– Quickly reverse the ball to catch the zone overshifted.

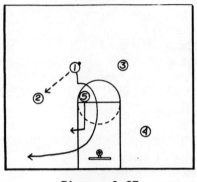

Diagram 9–37

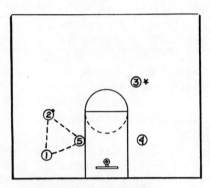

Diagram 9–38

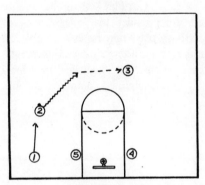

Diagram 9–39

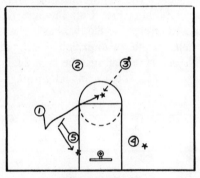

Diagram 9–40

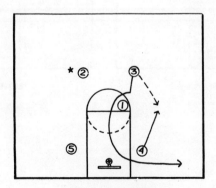

Diagram 9–41

Dribble Entry Play

When additional zone offense is desired, the Dribble Entry Play may be used. It starts as guard (1) dribbles at (2) and clears him down and around post man (5). This dribble rotates the front of the zone. See Diagram 9-42.

Player (3) then cuts over post man (5) to the basket. Against zones, (3) will very seldom be open on this cut. See Diagram 9-43.

However, as (3) cuts by, (2) steps to the point, receives a pass from (1) and reverses it to (3), who has looped around (4) and to the wing area. Player (4) helps (3) get open by pinning the nearest zone player inside. See Diagram 9-44.

If (2) can get the ball to (3) and he, (3), does not shoot, it keys the Flex and tells (1) to cut to the high post and form a triangle with (5) and (4). See Diagram 9-45.

If (2) cannot pass to (3), he passes to (1) and starts a Slash Cut Option by cutting off (5) and to the ballside corner. See Diagram 9-46.

From there, the passing triangle is maintained until (1) decides to change it by dribbling out front.

The Disciplined Flex Control Motion allows a team to control the tempo of the game. The stalling, teasing nature of the Slash Cut Play sets up the defense for a probing Flex Cut. Pressure relievers are provided that offer secondary modes of entry to the two basic plays. Auxiliary plays may be used to give the offense depth, or to exploit specific situations. With a few simple adjustments, this offensive plan may be used against zone defenses. It is an ideal plan for a team lacking a big man and wishing to play in a disciplined controlled fashion.

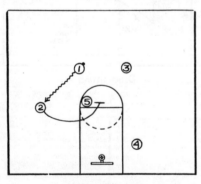

Diagram 9-42

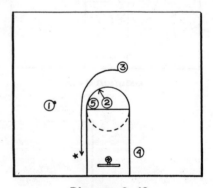

Diagram 9-43

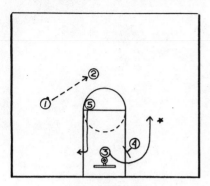

Diagram 9–44

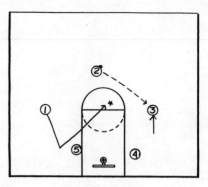

Diagram 9–45

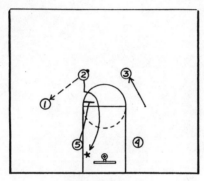

Diagram 9–46